Crisp, clear and challenging. Interlaced with h
a stimulating book.

Secretary for
International Fellowship of Evangelical Students

In this book, the message of Nehemiah, which is so relevant for today's church, is explained and applied with great skill.

Ian Coffey
Vice Principal (Strategy), MA Course Leader and Director of Leadership Training, Moorlands College, Sopley, UK

From confusion to confidence, from mourning to mending, from faith to action, God's Word brings purpose, hope and comfort to God's people in every generation. God's Word also challenges and warns against serious inconsistency, as well as a drift towards an easy religion and faith shaped by personal expediency rather than godly determination. The Langham titles on the books of Nehemiah, Habakkuk and James by Jonathan Lamb bring alive God's Word in a clear, faithful and relevant manner. They challenge us to live consistent, authentic Christian lives in a morally bewildered and spiritually confused world, with God's purpose and for his glory. I highly recommend them to you.

Rev Patrick Fung, MD
General Director, OMF International

We need sermons that are authentic to the text of scripture, lucid in conveying its truths, and courageous in applying the word of God to our lives today. In the expository ministry of Jonathan Lamb, you will find all of these characteristics, and the sermons contained in this book bear witness to this commendation. They once blessed a live audience and have since continued to bless many more people through the printed page, along with the additional questions and application. May your soul be enriched as you find the big questions of life answered from scripture in studying these passages yourself!

Conrad Mbewe, PhD
Pastor, Kabwata Baptist Church
Chancellor, African Christian University, Lusaka, Zambia

Jonathan Lamb at his heart-warming, challenging best. Life-changing stuff.
Richard Cunningham
Director, Universities & Colleges Christian Fellowship (UCCF), UK

Faith in the Face of Danger

Langham
PREACHING RESOURCES

Faith in the Face of Danger

An Introduction to the Book of Nehemiah

Jonathan Lamb

PREACHING RESOURCES

© 2018 by Jonathan Lamb

Published 2018 by Langham Preaching Resources
An imprint of Langham Creative Projects

Langham Partnership
PO Box 296, Carlisle, Cumbria CA3 9WZ, UK
www.langham.org

This book was previously published in 2004 by Keswick Ministries, UK. ISBN: 978-1-85078-580-4

ISBNs:
978-1-78368-891-3 Print
978-1-78368-387-1 ePub
978-1-78368-388-8 Mobi
978-1-78368-389-5 PDF

British Library Cataloguing in Publication Data
A catalogue record for this book is available from the British Library

ISBN: 978-1-78368-891-3

Cover & Book Design: projectluz.com

CONTENTS

Introduction

All around the world Christians are under pressure. It is now estimated that 90 percent of religious persecution is directed against the Christian community. Some two hundred million evangelicals in over thirty-five countries are subject to direct and hostile persecution, but there are very few countries where believers escape the pressures of a culture that is against Christ and his followers.

Throughout the story of Nehemiah, his personal faith – and that of the people of God – was under constant attack. This is reflected not simply in the hostile opposition that is recorded in chapters 4 and 6. It is also found in the subtle temptation to displace the priority of God's Word, or to lose sight of his greatness and holiness, or to live for selfish purposes rather than for the good of God's people, or to adopt the value system of their pagan neighbours instead of living according to the standards of the holy God who had called them to belong to him and who had brought them home to Jerusalem.

This is why the book has such powerful relevance for the Christian community today. For we too need to learn the lessons of trusting God and his Word in the midst of a raft of dangers, all of which are similar to those we will discover in the experience of God's people, back in the restored city of Jerusalem in Nehemiah's day.

This book is based around five Bible expositions given at the Keswick Convention in the UK. It is not intended to be a verse-by-verse commentary since several sections of the book of Nehemiah are omitted, but it seeks to expound key chapters, grouped around five main themes. It also retains some elements of the original preaching style but has been freshly crafted to help individuals and groups discover some of the wonderful themes from this section of God's Word.

The five expositions form the five sections of this book. In several instances, I have grouped Nehemiah's material in such a way to help us grasp the key issues of his memoirs. Chapters 3 and 5 are brought together, as they address what it means to be the people of God; then chapters 4 and 6 are dealt with together, as they explain the various forms of opposition that Nehemiah and the people encountered. Finally, chapters 10 and 13 are placed together, as they are clearly related in their emphasis on the importance of distinct godly behaviour.

There are also questions added throughout the book, which I hope will be helpful both for personal reflection and for group discussion. I am grateful to Langham Preaching Resources for making this title available to a wider global audience, and knowing the many preachers' clubs or fellowship groups that meet in country after country, I hope that the questions in each section will be useful for discussion in those groups. But the title is written for all believers, not just preachers, since we all face the challenge of sustaining our faith in the face of danger. Like Nehemiah and God's people in Jerusalem, we too can trust the God to whom we belong, knowing his gracious hand upon us whatever our circumstances.

Jonathan Lamb
Oxford, January 2018

Using This Book

As well as providing an introduction to major sections of the book of Nehemiah, the author has provided questions throughout each chapter as well as ideas for reflection and for further study. The questions help relate the principles explained in the commentary to our own lives and situations. You can use this guide either for your own devotional time with God or as a part of a group.

Using This Book for Personal Study

Begin by praying and reading through the passage and commentary a number of times before looking at the questions. You may find it helpful to note your answers to the questions and any other thoughts you may have. Putting pen to paper will help you think through the issues and how they specifically apply to your own situation. It will also be encouraging to look back over all that God has been teaching you. Talk about what you're learning with a friend. Pray together that you'll be able to apply all these new lessons to your life.

Using This Book in a Small Group: A Note to Group Leaders

In preparation for the study, pray and read the passage of Scripture and commentary over a number of times. Use other resource material such as a Bible dictionary or commentary if these are available in your country.

At the top of each chapter we have stated the aim – this is the heart of the passage and the truth you want your group to take away with them. With this in mind, decide which questions and activities you should spend the most time on. Add questions that would be helpful to your group or particular church situation.

Encourage your group to read the passage and commentary you will be studying each week before they come. Leave time at the end of the study for people to reflect and respond so that they are able to apply what they are learning to their own situation.

A Word to Preachers

The material in this book came from a series of five Bible expositions given in a setting with sufficient time to manage large sections of the book. If you are preaching through Nehemiah in a local church, it might be necessary to divide each section into smaller parts.

The key issue is to ensure we are handling a preaching unit – that is, a section of the book that has a clear theme, which can be explained and applied to a congregation in the time available. In this book, the five main sections include many sub-sections or smaller Bible passages, which would serve as a basis for preaching a longer series. It is important for preachers to work on Nehemiah and to make it their own. This book is just one way of dividing up the material in the exciting story of the rebuilding of God's family, and so it serves only as a guide to how this might be done.

This title is published by Langham Preaching Resources. There are Langham Preaching movements now established in many parts of the world. We encourage preachers to focus on three issues, and our hope is that these points are in some sense modelled in this study guide.

- First, *am I being faithful* to the Bible passage? Am I reflecting the meaning of the passage, so that I truly express what the original writer intended his original hearers to understand?
- Second, *am I being clear*? Is the way I present the preached message structured in a way that helps the listener or reader truly understand the force and flow of the passage?
- Third, *am I being relevant*? Am I connecting with the lives of my hearers, demonstrating how the Bible passage applies to the challenges of their personal, family and church lives, as well as the mood and worldview of their culture?

These are three good questions for anyone seeking to explain a Bible passage, whether in preaching, in small groups, or in one-to-one explanation of the passage to others. We hope you enjoy working on the passages yourself and determining how best to preach the Word in your own context.

Section 1

Choosing God's Priorities

Nehemiah 1 and 2

Choosing God's Priorities

Introduction to Section 1

When James Galway, the wonderful Irish flautist, was involved in a nearly fatal road accident, he was forced to evaluate what really mattered in his life. This is what he wrote:

> I decided that from now on I would play every concert, cut every CD, give every TV programme, as though it were my last. I have come to understand that it is never possible to guess what might happen next; and that the important thing is to make sure that every time I play the flute, my performance is as near perfection and full of true music as God intended, and that I shall not be remembered for a shoddy performance.

It often takes a crisis to force us to weigh what really matters in life. It might be our health, a bereavement, a personal tragedy – something which God uses to confront us with that basic question, "What is most important in my life?" It can also be a positive moment of crisis. Some years ago I stood in a small church in front of a packed congregation and was asked, "Do you take this woman to be your lawful wedded wife?" I remember the peculiar appropriateness (at least for my wife) of the text on the wall at the front, "Call upon me in the day of trouble and I will deliver you!" That kind of moment is a serious moment to assess priorities – "for richer, for poorer, in sickness and in health, as long as you both shall live."

Some people go through life without ever asking questions about fundamental priorities. To quote the actress Helena Bonham Carter, "We're all going to die anyway; so what does it matter so long as you keep a sense of humour and have fun?" That's today's philosophy: eat, drink, and be merry, for tomorrow we diet. Perhaps rather more seriously, the journalist Bernard Levin said that he hoped to discover why he had been born before he died.

So let me ask the question: What matters most to you? What really shapes your priorities in life? Is it your family, your bank balance, your career path, a certain relationship? What is it that motivates you?

Take a moment of quiet to reflect on these questions. It's not easy to assess our fundamental motivations and priorities, but try to be honest about what really matters in your life. Is how you spend your time reflected in these priorities?

The book of Nehemiah raises this fundamental question: What are the priorities for God's people? Once we have discovered those priorities, how can we be determinedly faithful in pursuing them? It is all about energetic purposefulness. It's about seeing what God calls us to do and then being committed to pursue that path.

This is extremely relevant because we Christians are constantly tempted to be diverted from those priorities. We face pressure from our own culture, which increasingly sees religion as something to be marginalized and privatized, until the gospel is gradually nudged aside as irrelevant and unimportant – simply a hobby for religious types.

Then there is pressure within the Christian community or even within our own lives. It's very easy for personal comfort and security to matter more than our desire to seek first God's kingdom. Self-fulfilment and self-indulgence sap our devotion and distort our priorities. There need to be moments when we step back from distractions, either in our culture or in our own lives, when we reflect prayerfully on what really matters.

Here in the book of Nehemiah, it was a sense of crisis in 445 BC that provoked Nehemiah and the people of God to assess what really mattered in their personal and community lives. They were forced to confront the priorities that were going to shape their national life and their distinctive witness as God's people. The opening two chapters of Nehemiah illustrate some basic priorities that governed Nehemiah's life in the midst of national collapse and spiritual decline. The first three chapters of this book examine three basic priorities that are essential if we are to exercise faith in the face of danger.

1

The Priority of God's Call

AIM: to examine what God's call will mean for us

Focus on the Theme

The idea of a call means different things to different people. Begin by asking yourself or your group what comes into your mind when you use this word. How is it used in general conversation? And what do you think it means to be called by God?

Read: Nehemiah chapter 1

Key Verses: Nehemiah 1:1–4

Outline:

1. Responsible Service

2. A Responsive Heart

The book opens with Nehemiah living and working in a foreign land. Artaxerxes is on the throne of Persia, and Nehemiah, the Jew, is there in exile, working as a top civil servant for the king. About one hundred and forty years earlier there had been a shift in the world's balance of power when Nebuchadnezzar, the king of Babylon, had destroyed Egypt, and his armies had moved into Syria and Palestine. Jeremiah, God's man at that moment, kept prophesying to God's people, warning them that unless they turned around from their unfaithfulness, God would send judgment from the north.

They refused to listen. Sure enough, God sent judgment, and the full weight of the Babylonian war machine moved in, crushing Jerusalem, destroying the walls, and carrying the people off into exile. It was the blackest moment in the history of God's people.

In due course, Persia became the dominant power, and during this period small groups of exiles began to return to Jerusalem, first under Zerubbabel, then under Ezra when the temple was rebuilt. (Ezra is a companion book to Nehemiah.) But still the city lay in ruins.

Chapter 1 begins with Nehemiah serving in Susa, the winter palace of the Persian kings, and we need to notice two important elements in the priority of God's call on this man's life.

1. Responsible Service

Nehemiah was born in exile, and like other Jews before him such as Daniel and his three friends, or Mordecai and Esther, Nehemiah rose to a significant position of influence, in his case, as a prominent civil servant in the court of King Artaxerxes. As he says, "I was cupbearer to the King" (1:11).

It's impossible to know what that responsibility really meant. Most think it included choosing and tasting the king's wine to check it wasn't poisoned. But he wasn't just a fall guy. He would have close access to the king as his protector and confidant. Xerxes, the father of Artaxerxes, was murdered in his bedroom by one of his courtiers, and so for Nehemiah to have been in this position means he must have been trusted as one of the top officials in Susa. Notice that Nehemiah's position and training in that pagan court was part of God's work in his life, equipping him for the challenge that lay ahead.

When he heard the distressing news of what was happening in his home city, Nehemiah was ideally placed to take action. There was no dramatic call, no divine vision, and no angelic messenger. He wasn't a religious professional, priest, or prophet; he was a civil servant for a pagan king, seven-hundred miles away from home. But here was a man whom God could trust, whose priorities were clear, and who was going to be central to God's work of rebuilding his people.

We know how important it is that in every country there are people committed to what we call full-time service, in their churches or Christian ministries. But there is a much bigger army to be deployed. Mark Greene, in a letter to supporters of the London Institute of Contemporary Christianity, wrote that there are about four million Christians in Britain, but only one hundred thousand Christian ministers. "If we want to win Britain, it will be done by equipping the four million for ministry wherever God places them. We will do it when the four million are equipped to bring biblical values to bear in discussions in offices and boardrooms and factories and hospitals."[1] It's true in every country, even where the Christian minority is very small.

Every Christian should be ready to take the opportunities right where God has placed them, to live for Jesus Christ in the now, not just in some hoped-for future. If you find yourself asking, What on earth am I doing in this job, this office, this factory?, it is important to see that Nehemiah was committed to responsible service right where God had placed him. Away from home, in a pagan court, as a follower of Yahweh, he might often have said, "What am I doing here?" We need to live for the Lord Jesus and for his kingdom values wherever he has placed us. We are each in a unique position to do that.

Are we in danger of making too strong a distinction between sacred and secular areas of work? What happens when this divide takes hold in Christian thinking?

Are there areas of frustration that you face at work? Is it possible still to see that you are in a unique position to serve the cause of Christ? What might be the particular ways in which your presence is significant for the cause of the kingdom?

---

2. A Responsive Heart

The second verse in chapter one introduces the news Nehemiah receives from his home town when a group of Jews arrives in Susa. We gain some insight about Nehemiah's concern because they don't volunteer the information:

> I questioned them about the Jewish remnant that had survived the exile, and also about Jerusalem.
> They said to me, "Those who survived the exile and are back in the province are in great trouble and disgrace. The wall

---

1. Mark Greene, in a letter to supporters from LICC (London Institute of Contemporary Christianity), details of which can be found at www.licc.org.uk. "At LICC we are committed to empowering Christians and church leaders to make a difference for Christ in our Monday to Saturday lives."

of Jerusalem is broken down, and its gates have been burned with fire."

When I heard these things, I sat down and wept. For some days I mourned and fasted and prayed before the God of heaven. (1:2–4)

The news was overwhelming and had a deep emotional and spiritual impact on Nehemiah. The message was clear: God's work was paralyzed, and God's people were demoralized. It's most likely that this was the result of the king's earlier order to cease rebuilding: "They . . . compelled the Jews by force to stop" (Ezra 4:23). It was a shattering blow for Nehemiah, not simply because of the disgrace of God's people, but because of what this represented: God was being dishonoured. Jerusalem was to be a "dwelling for my Name" (Neh 1:9); it was the holy city; it was the place where his presence would be especially known. Now, instead of its distinctive witness to God's glory and honour, instead of it being a light to the nations, it had become "an international joke," as one commentator puts it.

Nehemiah might have had a responsible job in Susa, with considerable security and prosperity, but he hadn't lost his spiritual passion. It's all too easy for us to lose our spiritual edge, to be indifferent about God's honour, but not Nehemiah. Such was his concern for God's name and God's honour, he mourned and fasted and prayed (v. 4).

In his account of the war in Bosnia some years ago, the war correspondent Anthony Lloyd indicated how easy it was to become desensitized to the appalling results of such inhumanity: "Brutal mutilation would stick in my eyes like a thorn for days, or else the expression or posture of a corpse would evoke sadness and anger within me. But as you lose count of the number of dead you have seen, a hidden threshold of sensitivity is raised, neutralizing most of your reactions."[2]

That's what happens to us Christians: our reactions to the appalling spiritual and moral decline that we see around us are gradually neutralized. We are living in a culture that has rejected God, but who would dream of even suggesting that we should dwell on, let alone weep over, the evil in our own hearts or the evil in our society or the spiritual decline we see in the church? Evangelicalism has very little place for tears.

I was interested to read recently that a TV news reader, Trevor McDonald, would sometimes spend some minutes weeping in his dressing room after

---

2. Anthony Lloyd, *My War Gone By, I Miss It So* (London: Doubleday, 1999), 6.

having delivered the national news. He felt something of the pain of the news he was delivering. When one of General Booth's workers was struggling to see any success in his work with the Salvation Army, he sent a telegram to Booth asking for advice. He received a reply, which contained just two words: Try tears.

It was that kind of responsive heart that was to be a foundation priority in God's calling of Nehemiah, and it is a foundation priority in our calling too – responsible service where God has placed us and a responsive heart to what God wants to do in the desperate situation in which we find ourselves.

Why is it that we have so little passion about the honour of God's name in our society?

How do we feel about the liberalism of the church, or the fracture lines within the evangelical family, or the rampant religious pluralism in our country? The majority of people are entirely indifferent to the Christian faith, or they are committed to non-Christian religions of various kinds. How do we feel about the fact that people are not worshipping Jesus?

Further Study

Take a look at how Jeremiah felt about the situation of his day described in Jeremiah 8:18–9:2. Try to capture his feelings by writing out this passage in your own paraphrase.

Reflection and Response

We have seen that God's call is not restricted to professional Christian ministry but includes God's purposes for every believer. Spend a while in prayer together for the different callings that are represented in your group – whether at work, in the home, or in the church.

2

The Priority of God's Purposes

AIM: to gain a deeper understanding of God's greatness

Focus on the Theme

What are the first things that come into your mind when you think about God's nature and character? Make a list of these, and ask to what extent these themes shape your worship and prayer?

Read: Nehemiah chapter 1

Key Verses: Nehemiah 1:5–11

Outline:

1. The Powerful God Who Fulfils His Plans (1:5)

2. The Faithful God Who Keeps His Promises (1:5, 8, 9)

3. The Holy God Who Requires Obedience (1:5–7)

One of the most significant features of the book of Nehemiah is the frequent reference to his praying. "For some days I mourned and fasted and prayed before the God of heaven" (v. 4). Chuck Swindoll calls Nehemiah "a leader from the knees up." His dependence on God was a vital priority in determining God's purposes for the work ahead. He was certainly an activist who got things done, and yet his first reaction on hearing the news was to commit himself to weeks of prayer.

What a lesson for our personal lives and our churches. When we confront a challenge, we are sometimes governed more by the maxim: "Why pray when you can worry?" He had received devastating news, and his godliness is reflected in the fact that he was committed first to discover the priority of God's purposes. There was nothing else he could do. No one but God could accomplish what needed to be done. If there is one great value in facing desperate situations where we have no idea what to do or how to respond, it is that we are forced to hold fast to God.

Abraham Lincoln expressed it like this: "I have been driven many times to my knees by the overwhelming conviction that I had nowhere else to go. My own wisdom and that of those about me seemed insufficient for the day." Nowhere else to go other than to God himself. That's just how Nehemiah felt, and it is a basic attitude we need to cultivate right through our Christian life and especially in our praying.

I recently read some correspondence in a newspaper about whether or not it was legitimate for Christian sportsmen and women to pray during their matches. Here is one of the letters:

> Sir, in an age where the winning is more important than the playing, I fear that professional sportsmen will continue to invite divine assistance. But we amateurs – like the vicar who, after holing in one from 300 yards, lamented that he would much rather have done it by himself – prefer to think that when there are moments of excellence they are produced entirely by our own efforts.

Christians face a subtle temptation: we would like to think that we fulfil God's purposes unaided. The book of Nehemiah is shot through with examples of this man's dependence on God, his devotion to God, his submission to God, and his desire for the glory of God. He had nowhere else to go.

What are the things on which we are tempted to rely in times of crisis or danger? Why do you think we are often so slow to turn to the Lord?

Verse 5 introduces us to a model of how to pray in a desperate situation. Nehemiah places the present challenge in the context of God's history of relating to his people with a mosaic of biblical references that form the foundation for his requests. There is great value in praying like this.

The prayers of the Bible are like the big clothes that parents buy for their children to grow into. I have a friend who says that when he entered secondary school his parents bought him a blazer, and it wasn't until a few months later that his friends realized he had hands at the end of his arms! Nehemiah's prayer, in common with similar sections of Scripture, contains profound truth that we can grow into as we use it as a model for our own commitment to discovering the priority of God's purposes.

Let's look at three features of the prayer:

1. The Powerful God Who Fulfils His Plans (1:5)

> "LORD, the God of heaven, the great and awesome God, who keeps his covenant of love." (v. 5)

"LORD, the God of heaven" – that's always the place to begin. He acknowledges the Lord, Yahweh, the personal God, the God of the Exodus who had saved his people (v. 10), and who had defeated their enemies. He bows before the God of heaven, the sovereign Lord who has universal supremacy. He is the transcendent Creator, the God above all other "godlets," as Alec Motyer once put it. This is the God who has the power to fulfil his purposes.

This is where Nehemiah begins. In fact, Nehemiah frequently makes reference to the powerful God, throughout his memoirs. He was constantly affirming this reality, as he focused on the sovereign Lord time and again. We find the phrase "the God of heaven" in chapter 1 (vv. 4 and 5), which is repeated in chapter 2: "The God of heaven will give us success" (vv. 4 and 20). Then his references to the Lord show something of Nehemiah's expanding vision: he is "great" (8:6), "great and awesome" (1:5; 4:14), and "the great God, mighty and awesome" (9:32). For Nehemiah, this wasn't theory. For the job he had to do this needed to be in his bones, deep in his heart. He declares that this great and awesome God is "my God" – a phrase that appears ten times in his memoirs.

In the building programme he was to lead, in the opposition he was to confront, in the reforms he was to introduce, he would depend on "my God" at every turn, trusting the great and awesome God. The reason for his dogged determination against all odds was that, like Moses, "he persevered because he saw him who is invisible" (Heb 11:27).

I often work among Christians in countries where the evangelical community is a desperately small minority, where human and financial resources are minuscule, and where the temptation to give up is a daily one. Some of us feel like this, and in such circumstances we need to be able to see the Lord, Yahweh, the God of heaven, the great and awesome God. It certainly makes a difference to the way we pray if first of all we raise our eyes to the great and awesome God, the God above all other "godlets."

A. W. Tozer once said that what comes into your mind when you think about God is the most important thing about you. But growing in our understanding of God's greatness doesn't happen automatically. In what ways do you think this happens?

---

2. The Faithful God Who Keeps His Promises (1:5, 8, 9)

". . . who keeps his covenant of love." (v. 5)

"Remember the instruction you gave your servant Moses, saying, 'If you are unfaithful, I will scatter you among the nations, but if you return to me and obey my commands, then even if your exiled people are at the farthest horizon, I will gather them from there and bring them to the place I have chosen as a dwelling for my Name.'" (vv. 8, 9)

One of the most distinctive ideas in the Old Testament is God's steady persistence in loving his people despite their extraordinary waywardness. That's what he promised, and he will remain faithful to that promise. The Bible uses the word covenant to describe that relationship, and Nehemiah's prayer is based on that foundation: God can be trusted. God will be faithful to what he has promised.

I heard a while ago of a Danish TV comedian who was elected to the Danish Parliament. He had an unusual manifesto. This is what he promised: better weather, a following wind for cyclists, shorter queues at shops, and he was campaigning for better Christmas presents. He attracted some twenty-four thousand votes. After being elected he said, "It was all a practical joke. Honestly. I guess people elected me because my promises are just as trustworthy as those of conventional political parties."

The covenants in the Old Testament were founded on God's sovereign grace. He had chosen the Jews; he had revealed himself to them; he had rescued them, and therefore he would not give up on them.

When we come to pray, we can be absolutely sure about God's ability to fulfil what he has promised. Nehemiah prays in verse 8, "Remember." It's a key word in his prayer vocabulary (4:14; 5:19; 6:14; 13:14, 22, 29, 31), and it represented a call to God to intervene. He is saying, "If you've been faithful to your promise in sending us into exile because of our unfaithfulness, now fulfil your promise to bring us back and restore us, as we obey you."

The same theme comes through in the prayer of chapter 9. "You have kept your promise because you are righteous" (v. 8); "who keeps his covenant of love" (v. 32). The prayer is saturated with that kind of covenant language – your people, our God, my God. We belong to you. Please be faithful in fulfilling what you have promised, "Restore, O LORD, the honour of your name."

There are many times when we feel we cannot pray because we are paralyzed by our sense of failure. We can't imagine that God would listen to us, let alone accept us back. It's then that these words matter: "You keep your covenant of love." However inadequate my faith, however slight my hold of him, God will not let go of me.

We need to remember that the greatest covenant of all is found in Jesus Christ. By faith in him we have been brought into a covenant relationship with the living God and with his global family, founded on God's grace. So when we pray, however inadequate that might be, we can come to God on the basis of his having chosen us, having welcomed us into his family, having saved us through Christ's work. We say the same as Nehemiah said: we belong to you; please don't give up on us; be faithful in keeping your promises. And that's why praying with the Bible open in our hands is so important.

When I feel paralyzed in my praying, I turn to a prayer like this one in the first chapter of Nehemiah or to some of the psalms that appeal to God. Spurgeon used to say that when we find it difficult to pray, "we shall find every attribute of the Most High to be, as it were, a great battering ram with which we may open the gates of heaven." Whatever our emotional or spiritual state, we can come to God knowing that his grace never ends. He is the faithful God who keeps his promises.

Discuss together some of God's promises in Scripture that have been specially encouraging in your life – particularly in the difficult times. Turn these promises of the Bible into prayers of thanksgiving.

3. The Holy God Who Requires Obedience (1:5–7)

> "LORD, the God of heaven, the great and awesome God, who keeps his covenant of love with those who love him and obey his commandments." (v. 5)

> "I confess the sins we Israelites, including myself and my father's house, have committed against you. We have acted very wickedly toward you. We have not obeyed the commands, decrees and laws you gave your servant Moses." (vv. 6, 7)

Having reviewed God's covenant promises, Nehemiah moves to confession. For this was also a covenant of human responsibility: obedience to God mattered. The judgment of God that had resulted in the destruction of Jerusalem was the result of their sin. So it follows that, if he was about to appeal to God for the restoration of the city and its people, it would have to be done on the basis of a confession of those sins that had led to its destruction.

Nehemiah doesn't distance himself; he identifies with the people and acknowledges his own sinfulness before God. There is nothing self-righteous or superior about him. Ezra was much the same. Discovering the unfaithfulness of the people, he fell on his knees and prayed, "I am too ashamed and disgraced to lift up my face to you, because our sins are higher than our heads and our guilt has reached to the heavens" (Ezra 9:6). This kind of solidarity is important. It's all too easy to criticize the church or distance ourselves from its failings, but when the Holy Spirit is at work, he will show us that we too are guilty.

If mourning over the state of our church and our country is one of the lessons of this chapter, then coming in confession to a holy God, who requires obedience, is part of that process. Nehemiah would only know God's blessing as he and the people expressed genuine repentance for their unfaithfulness.

One of the features most noted in accounts of revival is the awareness of the awfulness of sin and a willingness to confront it in prayerful repentance. As we hear the challenge of God's Word and allow the Holy Spirit to review our attitudes, our behaviour, our habits, our motivations, and our priorities, we too will begin to see sin as God sees it, and respond as Nehemiah did.

Finally, in an attitude of submission, he brings his request at the close of the prayer on the basis of the rock-solid convictions we have highlighted. He has prayed to the powerful God who fulfils his plans, the faithful God who keeps his promises and the holy God who requires obedience.

Now, in the context of renewed commitment, Nehemiah lays his specific request before God: "Lord, let your ear be attentive to the prayer of this your servant and to the prayer of your servants who delight in revering your name. Give your servant success today by granting him favour in the presence of this man" (v. 11).

Nehemiah had prayed day and night for months. What shaped the future was neither his diplomacy nor his political or administrative skill. It was his complete dependence on the God of heaven.

Holiness is a word that seems to be less frequently used in our Christian vocabulary. Why do you think that is?

Similarly, confession in worship often has rather less prominent a place than exuberant praise. Where do you think the balance should be found?

We are sometimes prone to criticize others rather than acknowledge our part in the church's failures. Nehemiah was not the only person in Scripture to identify with the failures of God's people – can you think of others? What lessons can we draw for our own attitudes today? (For example, look at Isaiah 6:1–10; Jeremiah 8:21–9:6; Romans 9:1–5.)

Further Study

Here are some biblical prayers – some big clothes to grow into. Spend a while reading them through, noting what they say about God's character and actions. Use them as foundations for your own praying.

Exodus 15:1–18

1 Kings 8:22–53

Nehemiah 9:5–37

Acts 4:23–31

Ephesians 3:14–21

Reflection and Response

Discuss together how our prayers today differ from Nehemiah's prayer. To what extent are those differences to be expected, and to what extent should we try to emulate Nehemiah?

Go back to the list of characteristics you made at the beginning of the session. Now that you have looked at Nehemiah's understanding of God, add to the list if you would like to, and then spend a while praying for each other on the foundation of these great attributes of God.

3

The Priority of God's Perspective

AIM: to see our situation as God sees it

Focus on the Theme

Can you recall times when you have stood on a hill, or been at the top of a tall building in the city, and had a panoramic view of the world below? What is it that is so liberating about that kind of experience? Do you think there is a spiritual equivalent?

Read: Nehemiah chapter 2

Key Verses: Nehemiah 2:17, 18

Outline:

1. God's Timing (2:1–9)
2. God's Control (2:10–20)

A story is told of an Oxford student who, nearing the end of his final year at university, wrote a letter to his parents:

Dear Mum and Dad,

I know you haven't heard much from me in recent months, but the fact is this. A few weeks back, there was a fire in the flat and I lost all my possessions. In fact I only escaped with my life by jumping out of a second-floor window. In the process of doing so I broke my leg, so I finished up in hospital. Fortunately, I met the most wonderful nurse there. We immediately fell in love, and, well, to cut a long story short, last Saturday we got married. Many of our friends say this was over-hasty, but I am convinced that our love will more than compensate for the differences between our social backgrounds and ethnic origins. By this time, Mum and Dad, I suspect you may be getting a bit worried, so let me tell you straight away that everything I have written in this letter up to now is false. I made it up. The truth is, two weeks ago I failed my final exams. I just want you to get this in the proper perspective.

Nehemiah was concerned to gain the proper perspective on the problems that lay ahead. I am sure that the same applies to every Christian. It is vital that we gain God's perspective for our lives, our calling, and our church. There are two specific features on which we will focus.

1. God's Timing (2:1–9)

Chapter 2 opens after four months of Nehemiah mourning, fasting, and praying. Gradually he had come to the point of formulating his prayer request of 1:11. Everything now depended on God's timing. Nehemiah was an activist, and his willingness to wait for God's time to answer the prayer is impressive. Any premature action on his part would have threatened the entire venture.

Weeks passed until eventually one day King Artaxerxes asked Nehemiah why he appeared so sad (2:2). Appearing mournful before the king was worthy of punishment, and commentators vary as to whether he deliberately decided this was the day to look mournful or whether, given the four months of fasting and mourning, it was inevitable that eventually the king would see the physical and emotional deterioration. Either way, Nehemiah was ready to respond to the questioning of the king.

Look at his carefully crafted answer: "May the king live forever! Why should my face not look sad when the city where my ancestors are buried lies in ruins, and its gates have been destroyed by fire?" (2:3). So when the king then asked, "What is it you want?" Nehemiah was ready to describe everything he needed to do the job of going back to Jerusalem, rebuilding the walls, and rebuilding the people (vv. 5–9). As well as praying, he had done his homework. He was dependent on God, but he was also ready to take the initiative.

There is no doubt that for many of us the waiting times are the most demanding periods of Christian discipleship. For anyone with an activist mentality, these four months of determining what might be God's will and of assessing when to act could have been a form of torture. But this is often the pathway God calls us to walk. Too often we imagine that prayer will provide us with a quick-fix solution.

In a letter to a newspaper many years ago, Fred Milsom wrote:

> Strangely the notion persists that prayer is simply asking God for things as if he were at our beck and call. Dean Inge once received a letter from a lady who said that she was daily praying for his death and that she had been successful on several previous instances. When, unaccountably, George Hirst was dropped from the English cricket team, prayer was offered at the Sunday night prayer meeting in a Yorkshire Methodist Chapel, "O God, open the eyes of the selectors." But it doesn't usually work, as all of us know who, after poor preparation, have prayed to pass examinations. Prayer is not a slot machine where you put your money in and get your chocolate out.

The process of prayer is one whereby we begin to think God's thoughts after him, to desire the things he desires, to love the things he loves. It is a process whereby we begin to see things from his point of view. The waiting time is often when God can make us what he wants us to be. This had been happening during Nehemiah's four months of prayer. It is in this context that his famous arrow prayer should be seen: "Then I prayed to the God of heaven, and I answered the king" (2:4).

It is rather like the non-verbal signals that two people might use who know each other very well. My wife just has to raise her eyebrows, and I get the message on what she thinks about my behaviour. People who have spent a long talking together can communicate swiftly like this, as in Nehemiah's prayer in verse 4. It was effective precisely because it grew out of a life of prayer. Nehemiah knew "my God" and was able to discern immediately that this was the moment for action.

That it was God's time is clearly signalled in verse 8: "And because the gracious hand of my God was on me, the king granted my requests." It must have been God's hand. The decision to allow Nehemiah to return and rebuild Jerusalem required the king to make a political U-turn. He had previously ordered that the rebuilding work should stop (Ezra 4:15, 21). Now he had to reverse his foreign policy. It's possible that the unstable political situation of the time meant that Artaxerxes saw the wisdom of strengthening Judah, providing a buffer state between Persia and a rather unstable Egypt. But even if it was a wise political move, it was still the hand of God.

A few years ago some of my friends were affected by a clampdown on religious activities in Azerbaijan. Following the intervention of the Norwegian defence minister, who was a Christian, the president of Azerbaijan completely reversed his policy on religious freedom, releasing pastors and granting requests to build churches. It was a political U-turn, and God is well able to achieve this if it is his purpose. There was much prayer and political intervention, but ultimately all of those concerned could say, along with Ezra and Nehemiah, "the gracious hand of my God was on me" (see also Ezra 7:6, 9, 28; 8:18; Neh 2:18).

It was the Lord, the God of heaven, who could cause the autocratic king of Persia to reverse his former foreign policy, and he is able to do that in the details of your life and mine, as well as in international politics. Many Christians struggle with the bewildering questions about the impact of evil, the opposition against churches, or the apparent delays in God's action in our family or personal life. In such circumstances we need to hold on to the priority of God's timing. He knows what is best. As Peter was to say to the hard-pressed believers of his day, "The Lord is not slow in keeping his promise . . . But the day of the Lord will come . . ." (2 Pet 3:9, 10).

Have there been times in your life when, looking back, you can see how God's timing was just right, even though at the time you found the situation difficult? Share these with the group and take a moment to thank God for his personal care for you.

Are there situations in your life or your church where you long for God's intervention, and where the waiting time seems too hard to bear? If you are able to mention these situations to others in the group, turn them into prayer together.

There are many parts of the world where our fellow believers will understand the title of this book – *Faith in the Face of Danger*. Share with one another any news you have of Christians under pressure, and pray together for God's intervention.

Take a look at some websites that give more information about Christians under pressure. For example:

- Open Doors exists to provide resources, training, and support for those who are persecuted for their faith in Christ. *www.opendoors.org*

- Christian Freedom International is a human rights organization that combines advocacy with humanitarian assistance. *www.christianfreedom.org*

- Barnabas Fund exists to assist persecuted Christian minorities by prayer and practical support. *www.barnabasfund.org*

---

2. God's Control (2:10–20)

Gaining God's perspective is vital in every area of our lives. We can be overcome with pessimism and discouragement or ignore the challenges and dismiss the opposition. We need to see things as they are and see things as they could be.

Within a matter of days of arriving in Jerusalem, the text tells us, "By night I went out through the Valley Gate toward the Jackal Well and the Dung Gate, examining the walls of Jerusalem, which had been broken down, and its gates, which had been destroyed by fire" (v. 13). Nehemiah was carefully assessing the need. He didn't rush into action, but wanted to be realistic about the challenge that lay ahead. With the circumference of the walls having been estimated at about two miles, the destruction was considerable. Massive stones that had tumbled down into the valley, blocking his way on horseback (v. 14), needed to be reassembled. As Jesus was to teach us, Nehemiah was counting the cost before building the tower, and that is part of the process in any work God calls us to do.

Such a perspective is also realistic about the opposition to God's work, which we will always encounter as God's people. Nehemiah hints at this in 2:10. He was in danger of upsetting the balance of power. Judah's neighbours had a vested interest in keeping Jerusalem weak. Verses 19 and 20 illustrate the confrontation that Nehemiah would face even more directly as the building work was to progress. They would face hostility at every turn, but the work in which they were to be engaged was the work of God. This is the shift of perspective we need when we are disheartened by the rubble or intimidated by the opposition.

Nehemiah says to his fellow workers, "'You see the trouble we are in: Jerusalem lies in ruins, and its gates have been burned with fire. Come, let us rebuild the wall of Jerusalem, and we will no longer be in disgrace.' I also told them about the gracious hand of my God on me and what the king had said to me" (vv. 17, 18). "The God of heaven will give us success" (v. 20).

He urges them to see things as they could be. He creates what we might call godly expectation: the God-given ability to see what could be, rather than just what is. This is basic to our work for God. George Carey calls a lack of vision "an ecclesiastical terminal illness." The dispirited people in Jerusalem needed more than the power of positive thinking. Their hearts and minds needed to be lifted to see what God could do. And we are the same. We need to be dissatisfied with where we are and develop a lively expectation of what, by God's grace, could be in our lives, in our churches, in our cause, or mission.

Nehemiah was to turn them from "the trouble and disgrace" (1:3 and 2:17) towards the "gracious hand of our God" (2:18). This attitude encourages "old men to dream dreams, and young men to see visions." It is Joshua saying to the people, "Get ready, you will cross the Jordan"; it is Nehemiah saying, "Come, let's rebuild the wall of Jerusalem." The critical turning point in the change of perspective was to see that God was behind the project. "The God of heaven will give us success" (v. 20). This is the fundamental priority we need in our own service for the Lord: it is God's work. It was the great missionary pioneer Hudson Taylor who said: "It's not great faith we need but faith in a great God."

Raymond Brown comments on the closing verses of chapter 2 by reminding us that what makes the difference for Nehemiah and his team is their doctrine of God: his transcendence and his imminence. His transcendence – "the God of heaven will give us success" (v. 20); his immanence – "I also told them about the gracious hand of my God on me" (v. 18). As Raymond Brown expresses it: "There is an eternal throne as well as a loving hand."[1]

---

1. Raymond Brown, *The Message of Nehemiah: The Bible Speaks Today* (Leicester: IVP, 1998), 58.

How can our vision – our godly expectation – be strengthened? How can we be sure that this is more than wishful thinking?

Why do the two themes of God's transcendence (his throne) and God's immanence (his hand) need to be held together?

Further Study

Read Joshua chapter 1. Try to identify similarities in the leadership attitudes of Joshua and Nehemiah. How did they each motivate the people of their day, and what lessons can we draw about how to encourage others within the Christian family?

Reflection and Response

We have seen how affirming God's timing and God's control are central to living our lives according to God's priorities. Can any of the group give an account of moments in their lives when, looking back, they can see how God's timing was significant, or God's control of events was especially evident? What do we do at those moments in our lives when it looks as though things are going out of control – and how can we renew our faith in the Lord's sovereignty in times like that?

Spend a while thanking God that our lives, our families, our churches – and our world – are all truly in his hands. Thank God for the "eternal throne and the loving hand."

Review of Section 1: Nehemiah 1 and 2

Think about the three main themes of this section, and try to summarize your responses as a group:

- The priority of God's call: are we serving God energetically wherever he has placed us? Do we have responsive hearts, ready to take up the challenge of God's work?

- The priority of God's purposes: are we committed to knowing God more fully, trusting his promises, obeying his commands, serving his purposes, believing in his power to change things?
- The priority of God's perspective: are we trusting him, his timing and his control, remembering the eternal throne and the loving hand?

Section 2

Building God's People

Nehemiah 3 and 5

Building God's People

Introduction to Section 2

Recently I met a Polish man who was living in Australia and working in Asia. He was returning home to Poland, and as we talked he described how he felt about his life, "I have no idea who I am or where I belong." It became clear that he wasn't referring to a physical or geographic disorientation but a much more deep-set crisis of identity and belonging. This is probably one of the most common complaints, not only in today's youth culture, but with people of all ages. There is a deep crisis of belonging. Many factors have contributed to this disorientation and rootlessness, but one of the most significant is the fracture of social relationships of all kinds.

In his book entitled *Love and Friendship,* the American social commentator Allan Bloom says, "Isolation, a sense of lack of profound contact with other human beings, seems to be the disease of our time."[1] In a recent survey of university students asked to identify their number one problem, 80 percent replied, loneliness. In my country, unlike those parts of the world where extended households are more normal, we suffer from a western disease: it is estimated that in more than 30 percent of British households, there will be a solitary person, 7.6 million separate units (or "civic atoms" as the jargon would have it). Add to this the statistics on divorce and family breakdown, and the picture is clear: the sense of emotional isolation and social alienation is a daily reality for many people. Few of us are spared the pain of fractured relationships. Even as Christians we sometimes feel that deep, in-your-bones, loneliness. It's no wonder, then, that those who wish to encourage the church in its task of mission urge us to reflect on the importance of one over-arching biblical theme: community.

To understand and live by the biblical teaching on true community will be counter-cultural today. If we live as we should as God's people, it will be deeply attractive in this world of social alienation. God's covenant formula, "I will be your God, you will be my people," is repeated throughout the Old Testament

---

1. Allan Bloom, *Love and Friendship* (New York: Simon & Schuster, 1993).

and is expressed in the New Testament in the reality of God's church, God's new society. This is the place where true community should be expressed.

We sometimes look at the book of Nehemiah as a wonderful book about leadership, and it is. But it would be a mistake to view it solely as the story of an individual. Its underlying theme is not so much the importance of leadership, nor the importance of the building of a wall. It is a story about the restoration of God's people, God's community.

Chapters 8 to 13 of Nehemiah express this in a variety of ways. In chapters 7, 10, 11, and 12, we find quite long lists of people, identifying who their ancestors were and which village they came from. We might wonder why such lists appear in biblical books, but this was all part of the process of defining identity and strengthening solidarity as God's community, now that they were back from exile.

The theme of building God's people is sharply focused in two earlier chapters in Nehemiah, to which we now turn. In Nehemiah 3 we will look at the community at work, and in chapter 5 at the community at risk. These chapters will highlight the fact that the theme of *Faith in the Face of Danger* has significant corporate implications for us as members of God's family.

4

The Community at Work

AIM: to learn more about how we can build Christian community

Focus on the Theme

Can you think of positive examples in your own experience of a sense of shared purpose that has made all the difference in your family, everyday work, or specific areas of Christian service? It might be anything from working together to build a wardrobe, to preparing for a trip, to developing a project at work. Describe to the group what made these experiences so positive.

Read: Nehemiah chapter 3

Key Verses: Nehemiah 3:1–12

Outline:

1. A Shared Purpose

2. A Cooperative Spirit

3. Committed Leadership

The task of rebuilding the wall was to become a major community enterprise. Just as important as repairing and rebuilding the wall and the gates of the city, the experience itself would bring together the fragmented community in

Jerusalem. Chapter 3 reveals several significant features of community building that are worth highlighting. They each have their contemporary parallel as we reflect on this issue: how do we build Christian community today? We will look at three key priorities.

1. A Shared Purpose

It's worth remembering that the exile had been a devastating blow for God's people. The destruction of the temple, the collapse of the city, the evacuation of the people – all of those events had called into question their status as the people of God. So the building programme that begins here in chapter 3 is, in reality, the beginning of the rebuilding of the shattered community, the people who belonged to God.

Rebuilding the walls would have several effects. First, it would be a testimony to God's power, as we have seen in Nehemiah's motivational speech in chapter 2, "The God of heaven will give us success" (v. 20). But second, it expressed their determination to be holy, distinct, separated from other nations in their faithfulness to God.

Gordon McGonville points out the importance of the walls as symbols. "Walls, like flags, can provide identity and solidarity. It is in these terms that we should view the present activity. The Lord was giving his people a badge, a further token – alongside the temple – that they were his people."[1] What is clear, as we read chapter 3, is the sense of solidarity, the shared purpose, the *esprit de corps*. They were working together wholeheartedly. They weren't just clearing rubble and carting rocks but were concerned with something far greater.

The story is told of the foreman on a building site who asks one of the builders what he is doing, to which he replies, "I'm breaking rocks." Then he asks the second man: "I'm earning for my family," he replies. When he comes to the third, with a glint in his eye he replies, "I'm building a cathedral." We all know that the object of our work radically affects the way in which we carry it out. If we are inspired we can put up with almost any inconvenience, overcome almost any obstacle.

For the people in chapter 3, building the walls was a testimony. This was a special city. Nehemiah had wept at the news of the disgrace of the broken city

---

1. J. G. McConville, *Ezra, Nehemiah and Esther*, The Daily Study Bible (Edinburgh: St Andrew's Press, 1985), 88.

in chapter 1. Now, the rebuilding of the walls was a reflection of God's glory. It was his city. It was his name that was to dwell there (1:9).

The shared purpose is acknowledged early on in the rebuilding programme. "Eliashib the high priest and his fellow priests went to work and rebuilt the Sheep Gate" (3:1). Up in the north-east corner this gate provided easy access to the temple and probably took its name from the sheep coming in for sacrifice. It is significant that Nehemiah began the work here, led by the priests, close to the temple. The verse continues: "They dedicated it." They consecrated this section of the work to God's glory. When the wall was completed, they celebrated its entire dedication, with marching and singing (12:27).

This was not just a construction project – "the people worked with all their heart" (4:6). They had a shared purpose in their hearts, they knew this was God's work and that it was for God's glory. It was this that inspired them, that energized their muscles, that pushed them forward in the rebuilding work.

In the twenty-first century, our circumstances are entirely different, but the principle here is extremely relevant to the building of Christian community. The effectiveness of the church's mission depends, in no small degree, on this kind of corporate solidarity and shared purpose focused around the Lord Jesus. As Paul says in Ephesians 2:21–22, in his metaphor of building, "In him the whole building is joined together and rises to become a holy temple in the Lord. And in him you too are being built together to become a dwelling in which God lives by his Spirit."

This kind of solidarity is constantly under attack, and all churches face the challenge of how to "keep the unity of the Spirit through the bond of peace" (Eph 4:3). One of the primary objectives of Satan is to attack this sense of shared purpose among Christians. He will do his utmost to disrupt any work of God by moving people away from their unified intention to do God's work for God's glory and will induce various forms of self-defeating chaos. In my experience of church life, it is often the smallest of things. Let me give some real-life examples from my church experience: disagreements over the colour you paint the walls of the church building, over the hymnbook you use, or even the way the seats should be put out. As surprising as it might seem, Christians are deflected from their primary task by exactly these kinds of trivial disagreements.

True Christian community will be strengthened when our purpose is clear, and we work together wholeheartedly to achieve it.

Can you think of typical distractions in the life of the church that prevent this kind of shared purpose? And what can we do about it?

We can't expect that there will be no disagreements within the Christian family, but how would the lesson of this section help us handle our differences and disagreements?

2. A Cooperative Spirit

As you read through Nehemiah's memoirs, you gain the general impression that all kinds of people are drawn together in achieving the one purpose. Throughout the chapter there are phrases such as "next to him," "next to them," and each person worked "side by side," irrespective of their background. The list in chapter 3 shows that forty different sections of the wall were worked on by people from different family units, different towns, different trades and professions, different genders, temple servants, district officials, priests and Levites. Nehemiah walks right round the walls and records that "the goldsmiths and the merchants" (v. 32) were working alongside the priests at the Sheep Gate (v. 1).

At certain points, Nehemiah clearly delegates responsibility to others, trusting them to oversee their section. "Next to him, the repairs were made by the Levites under Rehum son of Bani. Beside him, Hashabiah, ruler of the half district of Keilah, carried out repairs for his district" (3:17). This sort of team effort was essential to getting the job done, and almost all of them rolled up their sleeves and were willing to get their hands dirty. I saw a poster recently, which read: "Teamwork – means never having to take all the blame yourself!" Teamwork is basic to all Christian service.

It is essential in any church that we create a sense of community ownership. Leaders are called to equip others for their work of ministry, as Paul demonstrates in Ephesians 4. Every person, whatever their occupation, whatever their background, whatever their gender, is called to play their part. The ministry of mobilizing all of God's people is very much needed in our churches. It has been estimated that in the average church 90 percent of the work is done by 10 percent of the people.

Have you heard this parable?

One rugby team had a wonderful first season. There were only fifteen members of the club but all of them were players, and they won every match. However, after two or three years, two of them died and three moved to other places, so the team was now missing the front-row forwards and the centre three-quarters. But it continued to play on gallantly with only ten players. The club had now developed some spectators and an interested group would cheer on the brave team, although now they started to lose games, as might be expected as they were five men short. As the years passed, other players dropped out, so that in the end there was only a back row and two halves. However, there were now far more spectators. But as the team was ten men short, they always lost very badly, and for the most part the spectators jeered and criticized their lousy team.

Finally, the remaining players died or moved elsewhere, but the club continued to exist and to meet regularly to discuss rugby, though owing to the absence of players there were never any matches, although they frequently talked about the possibility of having one.

In the church there are thousands of spectators in the stands who badly need some exercise, and a small team of men and women on the field who badly need a rest.

The New Testament emphasis on Christian community calls for every-member ministry, a total participation of all those who are committed to the Lord of the church – all members finding their places on the wall, whatever their background, occupation, or gender, however young or old a believer they may be, and all working within that rich diversity to serve with their God-given gifts.

The purpose of leaders is to multiply, not to monopolize, ministry (see Eph 4:16). A central part of their calling is to work hard to liberate all of God's people, encouraging them to play their part in the building programme to which God has called us.

We often talk about every-member ministry in our churches. But how can we find our place within the church's mission?

Think about the different people involved in the work of your own church. In what ways can you encourage each other forward in service?

3. Committed Leadership

Along with the high priest and his fellow priests, several other community leaders and rulers are involved in the construction of the wall. That kind of leadership from the front is essential. The only discordant note in the chapter comes in verse 5, "The next section was repaired by the men of Tekoa, but their nobles would not put their shoulders to the work under their supervisors." Hugh Williamson notes that the verse could literally be read, "They did not bring their necks into service . . . the image is suggestive of pride (stiff-necked) rather than lack of enthusiasm."[2]

It was not simply that such work was beneath them. These particular nobles clearly resented Nehemiah's leadership. They had failed to capture the spirit of the enterprise: God's work for God's glory. Instead they were more interested in personal status. The attitude of the nobles is found in the church too. Again it works against true community.

It's found in a spirit of competition, or of status-seeking, or envy. Paul describes some of the attitudes he faced in Philippians 1. Some people were characterized by envy (v. 15): they couldn't stand someone being more successful than they were. There was rivalry (v. 15): they enjoyed belittling the work of others, imagining Christian work was a competition. Finally, selfish ambition (v. 17): the word has the flavour of canvassing for political office. These people weren't interested in the advance of the kingdom, but in establishing the power base for their own work.

This kind of church politics is very ugly, but Paul was able to rise above it. He was not concerned with prestige or personal glory. "The important thing," he said, "is that Christ is preached." That's the kind of committed leadership we need to display – not my reputation, my status, my position, my denomination, but the cause of Christ.

These three simple lessons are vital for the building of Christian community today, just as they were in Jerusalem then: a joyful commitment to the same

---

2. H. G. M. Williamson, *Word Biblical Commentary: Ezra, Nehemiah* (Waco, TX: Word Books, 1985), 196.

task, a willingness to work alongside others, and leaders who serve, support, and mobilize all of God's people.

Pride seems to have been at the heart of the problem for some of the leaders on the wall. What other attitudes do we find in our own lives that hinder us from working alongside fellow believers with a positive spirit? How can these obstacles be overcome?

Do you think we look for the same qualities of leadership in a bishop or church leader as we do a prime minister or business leader? Are there any qualities in Christian leadership that we would expect to be different?

Further Study

In Philippians 1:12–20 Paul speaks of the mixed motives of those who took advantage of his imprisonment. As you read the passage, make a list of the various things in the attitudes and actions of the people concerned (Paul included) that work for and against Christian community.

Reflection and Response

Studying this passage will have brought to mind your shared service in the local church. Think of some practical ways in which the qualities of community building that you have seen in Nehemiah 3 could be developed in one of the following situations. If the examples below seem too distant, choose an actual church project known to the group.

- Your church has decided to send a team to start a small church plant on a nearby housing estate.
- The youth team would like to run a holiday club for children.
- The pastoral team can see that large numbers of elderly people are not receiving the practical care they deserve.
- The leaders believe the time is right to prepare for a week-long evangelistic mission.

5

The Community at Risk

AIM: to see the dangers of division among God's people

Focus on the Theme

Many of us first became interested in the Christian faith through the influence of a friend or the warmth of a local church community. If you were like this, what were the things that impressed you about the person or the group that influenced you?

Read: Nehemiah chapter 5

Key Verses: Nehemiah 5:1–13

Outline:

1. Destructive Inequality (5:1–5)

2. Serious Inconsistency (5:7–9)

3. Honest Confrontation (5:10, 14–19)

4. Practical Solidarity (5:12, 13)

In Nehemiah 3 we saw how God's people were motivated to work together with a remarkable unity and sense of purpose. But Nehemiah now records an internal issue, which could have had very serious consequences not just for the life of the community but also for its witness to the surrounding nations. The whole enterprise of rebuilding the wall would have been of little worth if, at the same time, the people themselves had not been rebuilt into the true community of God.

What was the problem?

1. Destructive Inequality (5:1–5)

It is clear from these verses that this was within the family, in the community. The men and their wives raised "a great outcry against their fellow Jews." "We are of the same flesh and blood as our fellow Jews . . . but . . ." (v. 5). Something was happening that had the potential to create fracture lines and blow them apart. It focused around an economic crisis, and the opening verses show that there were three complaints surfacing:

Verse 2: Some of those working on the wall were very poor. They owned no land and had no source of income while they were in Jerusalem working on the wall, and so their families were gradually starving.

Verse 3: A second group is identified. They did have property, but they had to hand it over to finance houses, mortgaging their fields and vineyards and homes in order to pay for the increasing cost of food arising from the added pressure of famine.

Verse 4: A third group was having to borrow money in order to pay the taxes demanded by the king.

Verse 5: Indeed, such was the hardship that some families were having to sell their children into debt-slavery. "Some of our daughters have already been enslaved, but we are powerless" – the word enslaved could even have overtones of sexual abuse. The creditors were fellow countrymen, their flesh and blood.

Here we see the classic spiral decline into the poverty trap. The community that was to be known by God's name and declare God's values was treated with injustice and exploitation, and this caused an outcry. It was happening in the midst of the building project. In fact, it was not one community, it was two communities: the exploiters and the exploited, the powerful and the disadvantaged.

It is quite a contrast to the shared purpose and cooperative spirit in chapter 3, or the collective strength we will see in chapter 4. Now something had happened that was tearing the community apart. To set it into context, in terms of what the law permitted, the creditors were not acting illegally, but in the context of true community, the spirit of the law demanded something different. They were using a legal technique to redeem land for their own greedy benefit and were exploiting impoverished people who were part of their own community.

The simple point of application is this: selfishness and greed are enormously destructive of true community. The Old Testament prophets condemned these attitudes and practices. They recognized that greed, oppression, and injustice destroyed families and community. Poverty and debt led to appalling divisions among God's people. That's what led to the distressing cry, "we are powerless" (v. 5). As Chris Wright comments in his book on the ethical authority of the Old Testament, "This is a cry with some very modern echoes."[1] The powerless of many today, whether in society generally or even within our churches, arises from similar inequality and division.

In the New Testament, greed was not seen as some private vice. We tend to think what we do with our possessions is our own business. But take a look at 1 Corinthians 5:10–11. Here Paul lists the offenders who are to be excluded from the church. All of them have committed public or community offences – sexual immorality, idolatry, slander, drunkenness, swindling – they all have a community impact. But he includes in the list the word greedy – he mentions it twice. This is the person who refuses to do good within the family of believers. "Therefore, as we have opportunity, let us do good to all people, especially to those who belong to the family of believers" (Gal 6:10).

The attitude that insists on personal gain, but has no heart for the needs of others, is incompatible with the true sense of belonging among God's people, whether in the Old or New Testaments or in today's church.

"We are powerless." Are there individuals or groups within your own Christian community who might have such words on their lips? What might need to be done to change this?

Paul's list of community sins to which we have referred included the greedy. What do you think greediness is all about? In what ways does it manifest itself in churches today?

---

1. Christopher J. H. Wright, *Living as the People of God* (Leicester: IVP, 1983), 193.

2. Serious Inconsistency (5:7–9)

Nehemiah highlights the internal inconsistency of such behaviour within the community. "You are charging your own people interest!" (v. 7). These are your brothers. They're members of the family. He describes, with more than a hint of irony in verse 8, another element that is self-contradictory: "Now you are selling your own people, only for them to be sold back to us!"

The Jews were committed to do all they could to buy back their family members who had been sold into slavery to the Gentiles. They paid a redemption price in order to set them free. Now, after all of the efforts to buy back family members from foreigners, the creditors were setting up a new form of slavery, actually within the community itself. There was a serious internal inconsistency, and they knew it. Nehemiah's memoir states it succinctly: "They kept quiet, because they could find nothing to say" (v. 8).

Nehemiah presses his point still further, "So I continued, 'What you are doing is not right. Shouldn't you walk in the fear of our God to avoid the reproach of our Gentile enemies?'" (v. 9). The inconsistency within the community was clear. But what about the message it was giving to people outside the community? There was an external inconsistency.

Nehemiah is speaking once again about the honour of God's name. How the community behaved reflected on God himself. Nations around Judah would look at her behaviour and draw conclusions about the God whom they worshipped. Their community life was intended to be a radical challenge to the nations around them, so Nehemiah was right to imply that injustice, selfishness, greed – a lack of generosity and solidarity in community – invited criticism by the Gentiles and reflected badly on the name and reputation of God himself.

Of course, the same applies today. Any form of division within the Christian community not only impacts the fellowship internally, but damages our credibility in the eyes of a watching world. Once a minister was asked if he had an active congregation. "Oh yes," he replied, "half of them are working with me, and half of them are working against me!" He chose a humorous way to highlight a serious problem.

Some three hundred fifty years ago Richard Baxter wrote: "The public takes note of all this division and not only derides us, but becomes hardened against all religion. When we try to persuade them, they see so many factions that they do not know which to join and think it is better not to join any of them. Thus thousands grow in contempt of all religion by our divisions."[2]

There is a massive credibility gap when we affirm our unity and community and yet fail to demonstrate it in the realities of our lives. While this applies generally to the way we live as God's people, there is also the specific application of this passage to the issues of social and economic justice within the community.

In his book on the religion of greed, Brian Rosner records how, in the second century, a converted Greek philosopher attempted to characterize Christians of his day. He constructed a profile that demonstrated that Christians lived differently from the pagans around them in three obvious ways.

First, they didn't practise idolatry. Second, they didn't practise sexual immorality. And third, "If they see a stranger, they bring him under their roof. If they hear that any of their number is imprisoned or oppressed . . . all of them provide for his needs. . . . And if there is among them a man that is poor and needy . . . they fast for two or three days that they may supply the needy with the necessary food."

Rosner summarizes, "In the early church, the sharing of possessions was just as central to what it means to be a Christian as are [sic] the exclusive worship of the true God and the matter of sexual purity."[3]

We Christians need to see ourselves, not as a collection of individuals, with our separate priorities and needs, but as members of a community, the body of Christ, with all of its privileges and obligations.

The New Testament emphasis on the gift of hospitality meant more than entertaining one another at dinner parties: it was a commitment to help travellers, to provide somewhere for Christians to meet, and to care practically for the economically disadvantaged. The word hospitality literally meant "love for the stranger."

I have a friend who defines hospitality as "making people feel at home when you wish they were!" Of course, hospitality is costly, whether in terms of time or money or inconvenience, but generosity of this kind has a theological basis. You have been accepted by God, welcomed by him, brought into his family. Now show that same generosity towards others.

---

2. Richard Baxter, *The Reformed Pastor* (Grand Rapids, MI: Christian Classics Ethereal Library, 2002), 89.

3. Brian Rosner, *How to Get Really Rich* (Leicester: IVP, 1999), 132.

Can you think of ways in which non-Christian friends of yours have been impressed by aspects of Christian community they have seen – or issues for which they have legitimately criticized the church?

Is it realistic to think that the church really can be distinctive as a community? Are we any different from friends in a sports club, or regulars at the local bar? If so, how?

Can you think of people who are marginalized in the church, people who are hardly seen, but who need our care and hospitality? Discuss together.

3. Honest Confrontation (5:10, 14–19)

"I and my brothers and my men are also lending the people money and grain. But let us stop charging interest! Give back to them immediately their fields, vineyards, olive groves and houses, and also the interest you are charging them – one percent of the money, grain, new wine and oil." "We will give it back," they said. "And we will not demand anything more from them. We will do as you say." (vv. 10–12)

It is now time for action. Nehemiah swiftly calls for the immediate cancellation of debts and interest, and also the return of any property that had been used in repayment. There is an important issue here at the personal level, which says something about Nehemiah's leadership in the situation.

Nehemiah's memoirs not only show his willingness to confront failure, but also his positive commitment to generosity. Chapter 5:14–19 is another autobiographical section where Nehemiah describes his own motives and actions. Previous governors of the city, "placed a heavy burden on the people" (v. 15). This was their due as they ran substantial expense accounts because of their responsibilities. But Nehemiah declared that because the people were under such pressure, he would not do that but would cover the costs himself. He gives two reasons why he didn't take advantage of that situation.

First, "out of reverence for God I did not act like that. Instead I devoted myself to the work on this wall" (v. 16). In the light of his commitment to the God who had called him to rebuild the city and the people, he was determined to be different from other governors, those whom he describes as having "lorded it over the people" (v. 15).

Second, "I never demanded the food allotted to the governor, because the demands were heavy on these people" (v. 18). It was his sense of brotherly solidarity with the people that meant he refused to place any further burdens on them. He had the right to do so, but he preferred to carry the cost himself rather than add to the burdens of his fellow family members. You might recognize his two motives from Jesus's simple summing up of the law: love for God who called him to that work and love for others who belonged to the same family.

Our culture emphasizes rights more than responsibilities. What rights do we lay aside as we play our part in the church?

---

4. Practical Solidarity (5:12, 13)

Finally, Nehemiah calls the people to action. As the people agreed with his proposals to give back the land, to take steps to restore equality and to act generously, Nehemiah calls them to take an oath to do what they had promised (vv. 12, 13). This was vital for the well-being of the immediate task of building the wall. But more than that, it was basic to what constituted fellowship among the people of God. Community was the place of belonging, the place of inclusion and security. Nehemiah shakes out the pockets of his robe, as a simple visual aid – "in this way may God shake out of their house and possessions anyone who does not keep this promise" (v. 13).

We cannot escape the application of a passage of Scripture like this for our own day. Each of us will need to reflect on what it will mean for us, with our varied economic and social backgrounds, and the varied Christian communities to which we belong. But let me draw one or two conclusions:

First, equality and generosity arise from basic theological foundations. In 2 Corinthians Paul devotes two chapters to the question of the offering for the needs of hard-pressed Christians in Jerusalem. It was not just to meet needs; it was also seen by Paul as an expression of solidarity between Jewish and Gentile Christians. Practical financial help would be a clear signal of the unity of believers from different cultural backgrounds. Paul even called it "the privilege of sharing in this service to the Lord's people" (8:4). Unselfishness was the mark of true fellowship, expressed across national and cultural boundaries.

The early church, empowered by the Spirit, preached the love of God in Christ, in the context of a community committed to demonstrating that love. They certainly had their problems, but there was no sterile debate about evangelism and social action. The gospel found expression in powerful preaching, fruitful evangelism, extraordinary generosity to those in need, and a deeply caring Christian community.

Second, if we genuinely lived this way, we would be a powerful witness to a fractured world that is longing to see true community. Linked to this, there is the issue not simply of our solidarity within our own Christian community but also our solidarity with God's people worldwide. What of our global Christian community? To what extent are we genuinely committed to that? Do we respond in terms of practical fellowship and financial support?

Many Christian organizations try to balance limited resources, encouraging those whom God has blessed materially to help those who are struggling. We need to assess who are the equivalent of Jerusalem's powerless as we think about what true community will mean in our world, and we need to work to build strong partnerships worldwide.

As in Nehemiah's day, the kind of communities we build are a reflection of the kind of God we believe in – and that communicates. If on the one hand we declare we are the reconciled people of God, and yet at the same time we fail to display a community of generosity and equality, we are giving conflicting messages. True community arises from the heart of the gospel. It will be a radical alternative to the social alienation and isolation of our own culture.

It is interesting to note that Luke records at the end of Acts 2, "The Lord added to their number daily" (v. 47). What kind of community was it to which the Lord added people? "They were praising God and enjoying the favour of all the people." Just as it was deeply attractive then, this kind of community would be very magnetic in our society now. It's exactly the kind of community our world needs to see.

Take a look at 1 John 3:16–18. In encouraging practical action, why is John's argument so powerful?

What could Luke have meant when he said that the early church "found favour with all the people"? Is that possible today?

Further Study

2 Corinthians 8 and 9 is one of the most focused sections of Scripture about the grace of Christian giving. There are many different principles for giving generously outlined by Paul in these two chapters – make a note of them as you read through the two chapters, and think how they might apply to you and to your church.

Reflection and Response

As a group, can you think of a specific project you could adopt that would give some practical expression to the themes you have studied? It could be a small fund for a missionary, a child sponsorship scheme, a needy group in the community?

Review of Section 2: Nehemiah 3 and 5

Nehemiah 3 and 5 highlight both positive and negative aspects of Christian community. As you reflect on the dynamics of these two chapters, what are the issues within your own church that are positive examples of community building? Thank God for these, and pray about those areas of church life and unity that might be under threat.

As a group, why not consider writing a letter of encouragement to your church leaders? Or a letter of thanks to church members whose work is often unnoticed?

This section has also demonstrated that inequality can have a destructive influence in Christian community. What areas do you think need to be addressed in your own context, and how can the group respond positively to encourage a greater sense of true fellowship and solidarity?

Section 3

Knowing God's Protection

Nehemiah 4 and 6

Knowing God's Protection

Introduction to Section 3

During my first experience of sailing, off the Scottish island of Mull, the weather was quite severe and the boat was being blown over to what seemed like a forty-five-degree angle. That's one occasion when having one leg shorter than the other – as I do – was a positive advantage. Everyone else was falling over while I remained upright! We used the rather uncomfortable manoeuvre of beating: facing the wind and tacking in one direction and then another. It was painfully slow, but we were using the winds, which were against us, in order to make progress forward. I have often thought that this is a realistic model of biblical spirituality. Your journey forward in the Christian life is going to be contested all the way but, by God's grace, those very forces of opposition can be used by God to help you make progress.

When Paul was writing to the Thessalonians, he explained that, because of the pressures they were facing, he would send Timothy along to encourage them. Why? "So that no one would be unsettled by these trials. For you know quite well that we are destined for them. In fact, when we were with you, we kept telling you that we would be persecuted. And it turned out that way, as you well know" (1 Thess 3:3–4). You are destined for trials, Paul says. John Calvin, the influential theologian and reformer, commented on this verse that it was almost as if Paul was saying, "You are Christians on this condition – you will face trials."

The early Christians knew this. Luke's story in the book of Acts is often seen as an account of two movements: the movement of the Holy Spirit in establishing the church, and the movement of the powers of darkness that oppose it. So it is today. All who are involved in the work of God will find themselves under ceaseless pressure to give up. They will confront opposition from all kinds of sources, from outside and inside the Christian community.

It's as well to be honest about this. There is a danger of a form of triumphalism that suggests that Christians should always be riding high on a success-oriented spirituality. The Christian life, in these terms, is one of perpetual positive self-fulfilment. If that is your model of the Christian life, then as soon as you encounter struggles, you either become disillusioned, feeling God has let you down; or you become despairing, feeling that you have failed and have let God down – there must be something wrong with your faith if progress is so demanding.

All who are seeking to fulfil God's purposes, to run the race to which he has called them, will find themselves confronting one hurdle after another. Difficulties are not a punishment, they are an affirmation, and they are to be expected. When we become Christians, we undergo a radical change of allegiance. We are taken out of one kingdom – the kingdom of darkness – and transferred into the kingdom of God's dear Son. Neutrality is impossible. If now we are in God's kingdom, living by God's values, we will inevitably be in conflict with a world that is hostile to God.

It would be easy to become paranoid with fear if this was our only perspective of the journey ahead. Jesus balances realism with assurance when he says to us in John 16:33, "In this world you will have trouble." That's the reality. There's no avoiding that kind of confrontation. "But take heart! I have overcome the world." He assures us that in this struggle we will enjoy God's protection. The opposition, however determined and hostile, ultimately has no other expectation than final defeat: "I have overcome the world."

The book of Nehemiah begins with a man and a people devoted to a God-given task. They see it as an absolute priority and carry it out with determination. So it is no surprise that the story should soon include an account of the relentless opposition they faced. God's work is always resisted.

In Nehemiah's case, the opposition came at both the personal and the community level. Chapters 4 and 6 identify not only the various forms of attack, but also the specific responses of Nehemiah and the people in countering them.

6

When the Going Gets Tough

AIM: to confront the varied challenges to God's work

Focus on the Theme

What do you find most difficult about living the Christian life? Discuss together the different pressures we face as God's people.

Read: Nehemiah chapter 4

Key Verses: Nehemiah 4:1–12

Outline:

1. Hostility from God's Enemies (4:1–9)

2. Defeatism among God's People (4:10–12)
    a. Discouragement
    b. Intimidation
    c. Pessimism

Nehemiah's opponents have already been introduced in chapter 2. They were "very much disturbed" (v. 10), and seemed to be amused that Nehemiah was attempting to rebuild the walls (v. 19). But now, as the teams of workers are organized and motivated, and the walls are beginning to rise, the opponents view the matter more seriously. Sanballat "became angry and was greatly incensed" (4:1).

There were several reasons why opposition was surfacing. Personal ambition and jealousy were doubtless part of it, but one obvious reason was to do with economic power. One of the major trade routes of the day passed through Jerusalem, and a restored city would mean the loss of economic supremacy for Sanballat, the Samarian governor. The neighbouring provincial governors clearly did not like the idea of their economic and political status being threatened. Sanballat did not want to see Jerusalem become strong again, so he and his allies were determined to put a stop to the reconstruction programme.

1. Hostility from God's Enemies (4:1–9)

They started with ridicule. "What does this bunch of poor feeble Jews think they are doing? Do they think they can build the wall in a day if they offer enough sacrifices? Look at those charred stones they are pulling out of the rubbish and using again!" (v. 2, NLT). This was the beginning of a sustained propaganda campaign, and the fact that Sanballat spoke "in the presence of his associates and the army" (v. 2), suggests that he was addressing them, as much as the Jews, building his own support base of opposition. The audience would get the message: these were miserable Jews, good for nothing, incapable of turning this heap of rubble into any kind of lasting fortress. The crowd would have loved it – you can almost hear the snickers and the taunts.

One of Sanballat's close allies, Tobiah, adds to the ridicule: "That stone wall would collapse if even a fox walked along the top of it" (v. 3). His sick joke was meant to imply that the opposition hardly needed to lift a finger. Foxes usually lived in ruins, and it only needed one of Jerusalem's foxes to trip lightly across the newly constructed wall to do the job for them. Archaeological research has indicated that Nehemiah's walls were up to nine feet thick, so it was a foolish thing to say, but the opposition was resorting to psychological warfare in this early stage of their attack.

This kind of ridicule impacts people differently. When the prophet Jeremiah faced this kind of mockery, he felt it keenly, as we see from his black writing in Jeremiah 20:7–18, and for God's people building the wall, it was sure to have taken its toll. They were facing a colossal task with limited resources, taking on a project that already had a history of failure. Ridicule wouldn't have been easy to cope with.

Mockery, hostility, and contempt towards the Christian faith are common in many parts of the world and will increase if we are faithful in proclaiming the exclusive claims of Jesus Christ. It might be the gentle mockery of people in the family or in the office; it might be jokes about our Christian lifestyle, or it might be direct hostility by those who object to our Christian commitments and Christian values.

Nehemiah's response to the sarcastic ridicule is recorded in verses 4 and 5, to which we will return in a moment. But the people pressed ahead with the work. "We rebuilt the wall till all of it reached half its height, for the people worked with all their heart" (v. 6). At the point when the people saw the progress, the opposition gained momentum. The enemies "plotted together to come and fight against Jerusalem and stir up trouble against it" (v. 8).

Hostility was brewing and Nehemiah introduces the opponents in verse 7:

- Sanballat, who had a Babylonian name and was Governor of Samaria, was in the north.
- Tobiah, who had a Hebrew name, probably ruled over the Ammonite territory to the east.
- The Arabs, who were Judah's southern neighbour.
- The Ashdodites, who were in the west.

Jerusalem was completely surrounded by the four neighbouring provinces of the Persian empire, and this unholy alliance, united in its opposition to the people of God, encircled them and intensified their threats. Whether or not they would have carried out their intention is debated, but the hostile threat had to be taken seriously.

Some of my friends working in Jerusalem recently set up a stand in the main university forum in the Hebrew University of Jerusalem to display and give out free literature, New Testaments, and copies of the video, *Jesus*. They were quite nervous about going public, and they received a mixed reaction. Some were fascinated and were very open, others were furious and offended, tearing up their literature, and one man decided to vent his anger for four hours. Here is how my friends recounted the situation.

> Amazingly he never grew tired of yelling, but the student group got an excellent rotation system in order, and took turns in taking his insults! On the last night, we held a discussion evening where students could come and ask a panel of believers any questions. A large group of religious men came, armed with all kinds of specific questions trying to draw out inconsistencies that they believed existed in the New Testament. It was a pretty exhausting night for all those involved. After the official discussion had ended, many small groups continued to talk until we were eventually asked to

leave the building just before midnight. We are very glad to have a second opportunity for a booth later this month.

These courageous young believers were determined to proclaim the name of Jesus despite hostility. It must have been tough for the people on Jerusalem's wall in Nehemiah's day, as they sought to be true to their calling despite the surrounding enemy.

Does anyone in the group have a story to tell of how they have experienced this kind of mockery or hostility? Describe how it feels, and how you have coped.

Does opposition make you want to throw in the towel, or does it challenge you to complete the task?

What kind of opposition does your group or your church face in its regular ministry?

---

2. Defeatism among God's People (4:10–12)

While the external attack gathered momentum, something was happening among God's people, which represented another form of pressure for Nehemiah. There were three problems: discouragement (v. 10), intimidation (v. 11), and pessimism (v. 12).

a. Discouragement

> Meanwhile, the people in Judah said, "The strength of the labourers is giving out, and there is so much rubble that we cannot rebuild the wall." (v. 10)

Discouragement was understandable. As verse 6 indicates, they were halfway through the project and that's always the most difficult moment. Quite recently a friend of mine commented on a remark in a cookery book he was using. He was preparing pork chops with cream and mushrooms, and there was a comment in the middle of the preparation process where the writer made the encouraging aside: "Don't worry – it always looks awful at this stage."

It's often true in our work. Halfway through you have neither the benefit of your initial enthusiasm nor the motivation of seeing the finished product. It is the toughest time to sustain your work and energy. It is similar to climbing a mountain. After the initial burst of energetic enthusiasm, you see rise after rise in the distance and no sight of the summit, and you soon draw the conclusion that you stand no chance of making it.

The people on the wall were overwhelmed with tiredness (the word for strength giving out means stumble, or totter). They were carting huge rocks day and night and were completely disheartened by the mounds of rubble that still lay all around them.

Are you close to throwing in the towel? It's a very common experience. A high proportion of missionaries brought home for health reasons, such as emotional exhaustion, face similar occupational hazards to those that David Livingstone confronted over one hundred sixty years ago. A medical correspondent recently commented on the research published by the British Journal of Medical Practice, following a survey of some two hundred British missionaries.

> Livingstone was often deeply depressed. Between 1853 and 1856 he suffered thirty attacks of malaria, and his wife died of the disease on the Zambezi river when she was forty. By the time Stanley found him, he was worn out mentally and physically, his supplies had been stolen and he had no medicines. He was almost at the end of the road.

We can't escape such feelings of physical, emotional, and spiritual exhaustion. In the midst of a particularly demanding stage in our work, one of my colleagues said, "The only thing holding me together is perpetual motion!" In other words, if she stopped, she would collapse. All of those committed to making a difference for the Lord in their personal witness, whether in evangelism or in living by Christian values and standards, will find they frequently feel the exhaustion of fighting on the front.

Can you imagine how Nehemiah must have felt? Outside the wall (that was still unfinished), ridicule and threats were within earshot, and the possibility of guerrilla tactics and terrorist incursions were considerable. Inside the wall, he now faced the despairing complaints of his own team.

Sometimes this kind of discouragement is one of the greatest weapons of the enemy. Jim Packer talks about the problem of "attitudinal rubble" in the church.

Pastors and spiritual leaders today, whose concerns extend beyond maintenance to mission, and who seek a genuine extending of God's kingdom, find themselves faced again and again with what has to be classed as attitudinal rubble – laziness, unbelief, procrastination, cynicism, self-absorption, in-fighting and fence-sitting among the Lord's people, and many similar factors that hinder and obstruct spiritual advance.[1]

b. Intimidation

Also our enemies said, "Before they know it or see us, we will be right there among them and will kill them and put an end to their work." (v. 11)

The intimidation took its toll. The people of Judah were taken in by the whispering campaign of the enemy, injecting a continuous stream of propaganda. This was gnawing away at their morale and steadily undermining their confidence. It is the kind of thing Satan exploits in our lives too, whispering in our ears, accusing us, exploiting our weaknesses, predicting failure, lying about God's promises. Facing determined opposition is exhausting. We can easily become paralyzed in the face of intimidation.

c. Pessimism

Then the Jews who lived near them came and told us ten times over, "Wherever you turn, they will attack us." (v. 12)

Pessimism within the community should have been no surprise. The prophets of doom, who are found in every group of God's people, were living in the nearby villages, undoubtedly under threat themselves, and they began to urge the people in Jerusalem to abandon the sinking ship before it was too late. It's a doomed city, they said. "Wherever you turn, they will attack us" (v. 12). Give up now. You'll never make it.

When I travelled to East Germany during the Communist period, I heard a joke that was one of many that helped people keep their perspective: What's the difference between an optimist and a pessimist? A pessimist says, "Things can't possibly get any worse." But an optimist says, "O yes they can!" I'm sure

---

1. J. I. Packer, *A Passion for Faithfulness* (London: Hodder & Stoughton, 1995), 108.

you've met such Christians. They have a special ministry of discouragement in the church, making it their mission to show us it can't be done. With friends like these, I am sure Nehemiah thought, "Who needs enemies outside the wall?"

Alongside the growing pressure on Nehemiah and the community, Nehemiah chapter 4 shows us how they responded to the opposition. Seven times in chapters 4 and 6, Nehemiah makes a journal note that reflects his dependence on God. We will turn to this in the next chapter, learning how we should respond as we face hostility from enemies and defeatism among God's people.

One of the most generous-hearted leaders in the early church was Barnabas, the "son of encouragement" (Acts 4:36). What do you think constitutes the ministry of encouragement in the church?

Further Study

Consider some of the examples of opposition in the early church, recorded by Luke in such passages as Acts 4:1–22; 5:17–42; 8:1–8; 19:8–20. How do the Christians respond in each of these accounts, and what lessons would you draw for your own Christian life?

Reflection and Response

Think about people in your church who are under pressure in their family or their work because they are committed Christians. And perhaps someone in the group will know of churches in other parts of the world where hostility towards their faith is a daily feature of life. Talk a little about what this must be like for them, their families, and their physical, emotional and spiritual well-being. Then pray together for some of the people you have mentioned.

7

Remember the Lord

AIM: to learn the most important strategies for handling opposition

Focus on the Theme

Discuss together some specific occasions when you have felt under pressure. What have been the things that have helped you to cope?

Read: Nehemiah chapter 4

Key Verses: Nehemiah 4:4–9

Outline:

1. He Remembered God's Justice (vv. 4, 5)

2. He Remembered God's Protection (v. 9)

3. He Remembered God's Power (vv. 14, 15)

4. He Remembered God's Commitment (v. 20)

As we read the story of the rebuilding it is not hard to see that Nehemiah was an activist, someone keen to press ahead with the job and capable of mobilizing others. But significantly in this chapter, the text shows how Nehemiah constantly returned to the God of heaven, the one who had called him to the task. In facing opposition, this was his default position.

There are four characteristics of the God of heaven that Nehemiah calls to mind.

1. He Remembered God's Justice (vv. 4, 5)

> "Hear us, our God, for we are despised. Turn their insults back on
> their own heads. Give them over as plunder in a land of captivity.
> Do not cover up their guilt or blot out their sins from your sight,
> for they have thrown insults in the face of the builders." (vv. 4, 5)

Nehemiah's prayer has provoked some disagreement among commentators. Is it a model of how we should respond to enemies? Doesn't it introduce a rather jarring note in the story? Surely Jesus taught us to respond in a very different way in his Sermon on the Mount (Matt 5:43–48)? Didn't Paul urge us to bless, not to curse, those who persecute us?

Of course, that's true. But at the same time, we should recall that such prayers in the Old Testament reflect an attitude of concern for God's honour. When the enemies oppose the workers on the wall, they are, in reality, opposing the work of God. It is his name that is being mocked, his cause that is being slandered.

What do we make of this kind of prayer? The imprecatory psalms (that include a spoken curse) and the prayers of Nehemiah and Jeremiah are expressions of anger at the fact that men are shaking their little fists at God, expressions of longing that God would vindicate himself. They are concerned for God's honour. Nehemiah saw that God's name was being mocked and his cause being slandered. So when we see these expressions of anger, we understand they are appeals for God to be true to his name and nature, to act justly and demonstrate his universal authority.

When Jesus faced enemies who insulted him, as Peter wrote, "he entrusted himself to him who judges justly" (1 Pet 2:23). When we are facing the hostility of God's enemies today, we can be sure of God's justice being ultimately fulfilled. In Psalm 73, the psalmist couldn't understand why God had allowed the apparent success of the arrogant and wicked who opposed him, "until I entered the sanctuary of God; then I understood their final destiny" (v. 17). When he came into God's presence and realized that God is the judge of all, he remembered what would happen in the end. So, whatever the opposition we face, we can be absolutely sure that God's justice will be done; his purposes will not be defeated.

Is it ever right to fight back or to defend ourselves as Christians? And what should be our motive if we decide to do so?

Psalm 73 encourages us to take a long-term perspective. Can you think of situations in your own life where this might help?

2. He Remembered God's Protection (v. 9)

"But we prayed to our God and posted a guard day and night to meet this threat."

Knowing that this was God's work, Nehemiah sustained his praying, and encouraged the people to join him. "We prayed to our God" – they knew that he would protect them from their enemies. We shouldn't underestimate the importance of praying for protection in our own lives and for Christian ministries. Perhaps, like me, you are grateful for people who pray for you and for your family regularly. I am so thankful for the commitment of good friends who ask the Lord daily to protect me on my travels and to provide for our ministry.

I recently read a report from Central Africa about a young Hutu pastor and his family who, when Tutsi soldiers broke into their house, asked if they could pray before they died. After praying, the family slowly stood up and saw that the soldiers were gone; not only out of their house but away from their village as well. Later, one of the Tutsi soldiers who had been there, came into a church and gave this testimony:

> You see, I was there when we broke into your house. I was the one who had your children lined up in my gun sight as you knelt and prayed . . . when suddenly a wall of fire, fierce and ferocious, jumped up and surrounded you. We couldn't even see beyond the flames. Due to the intense heat we knew the house would burn down so we fled. When we went outside and saw the house consumed by fire yet not destroyed, we fled the village as well. Later I realized this was a fire sent by God. If this is how your God responds, I want to know him too. I am tired of the fighting and killing. This is why I came tonight.

I could also recount stories of colleagues who have lost their lives for the cause of Christ in the last few years. We Christians carry no immunity from suffering or martyrdom, and we cannot fathom the mysteries of why God might appear to intervene on some occasions and not others. We have to trust his good purposes. The list of heroes of faith in Hebrews 11 demonstrates that some were snatched from the jaws of death, and some were sawn in two; both equally trusted God. This is all part of the mystery.

But what we do know is that we are encouraged to seek God's protection. In the light of the pressures on families, on Christian leaders, on committed evangelical ministries, on active churches around the world, God's protection is something for which we should pray daily. We are encouraged to seek God's protection and not take it for granted.

How can we be "alert to Satan's devices" without at the same time becoming paranoid?

Can you give an example of how you have seen God's care and protection in your life?

---

3. He Remembered God's Power (vv. 14, 15)

"After I looked things over, I stood up and said to the nobles, the officials and the rest of the people, 'Don't be afraid of them. Remember the Lord, who is great and awesome, and fight for your families, your sons and your daughters, your wives and your homes.'"

Nehemiah uses the language of his prayer in chapter 1 to encourage the people to refocus on the God of power, the sovereign Lord who achieves his purposes. That kind of thoughtful reflection puts the opposition into perspective.

For the Christian, calling to mind what God has achieved through Christ provides the perspective for our spiritual warfare. Colossians 2 gives us a wonderful mandate for our praying, reminding us that the certainty of victory in the warfare is absolutely guaranteed because of Jesus and his cross.

"And having disarmed the powers and authorities, he made a public spectacle of them, triumphing over them by the cross" (2:15). The picture is of evil spirit powers – "terrorists from hell" – stripped of their weapons. On the cross Jesus defeated every evil power, he triumphed over his enemies, set captives free and destroyed the captor. We are not free from our struggle with hostile forces, but we know the final outcome of the battle is absolutely sure. What Jesus did on the cross means that the opposition forces face final ruin.

It's rather like watching a video replay of a football match you know your team won. You are tempted to believe the opposition will score and win, but you already know the result. And as believers, we too know the outcome of our struggle. We are to keep alert to Satan's devices, but most of all we are to keep our eyes on Jesus, on the risen Lord who has defeated death.

Satan, the principalities and powers, and death itself have no other expectation than final ruin. The focus of that victory in our lives, and in our universe, is the Lord Jesus, crucified in weakness and raised by God's power. As theologian Fred Bruce once said, "We are not fighting for a position of victory but from a position of victory."

How would you answer someone who suggests that, because of Christ's finished work on the cross, there is nothing for us to do?

---

4. He Remembered God's Commitment (v. 20)

"Wherever you hear the sound of the trumpet, join us there. Our God will fight for us!"

In the midst of the pressure, this verse suggests that now the people have a new purposefulness about them, a new courage. This is God's work and, as verse 20 suggests, he is committed to see it through. He is guaranteeing the outcome. "Our God will fight for us!"

Nehemiah's response to the various attacks was to lift his eyes to heaven: to remember the Lord's justice, protection, power, and personal commitment. But there is one other feature of the passage to notice. At several points in the text we see the characteristic feature of Nehemiah's spirituality – the combination of prayer and action. So alongside the call to remember the Lord, we should note one other feature of their response: "But we prayed to our God and posted a guard day and night to meet this threat" (v. 9).

Taking various precautions and concentrating their defences, the people strengthened their sense of solidarity in fighting for one another; they developed an attitude of war alert and were constantly vigilant (vv. 16–18). Not only were they ready for any attack; they were watching the vulnerable places, the lowest points on the wall (v. 13), those points of weakness that needed special care. They even kept their clothes on through the night rather than wearing pyjamas (v. 23), so as to be sure they could respond to any attack at any time!

As we pray for God's protection, we are not to remain passive. Paul encourages us in Ephesians 6 to "Put on the whole armour of God, so that you can take your stand against the devil's schemes" (v. 11). This is no game: we need to be equipped, to be ready to use the weaponry that God has provided for us. We need to trust God's Word and Spirit in our lives, keeping alert to Satan's devices and standing alongside one another in the battle, praying in the Spirit. "Be strong in the Lord and in his mighty power" (6:10).

Take a few moments of quiet to reflect on the vulnerable points in your own life – the areas of potential weakness or temptation.

In what ways can you build up the defences at that point?

What parts of the Christian's armour do you especially need? Seek the Lord's help as you ask him to equip you to make progress in this specific area.

Further Study

Read Ephesians 6:10–19. What does each part of the armour of God represent practically? What do you learn from Paul's own example in this passage?

Reflection and Response

Nehemiah's response to opposition is to keep his eyes on the Lord. Is that our automatic response? How could it become a more natural part of our Christian life? What practical things would help us follow this example more seriously?

Opening a subject like this is sure to have raised some challenging issues or opened some old wounds. Pray together for the Lord's presence and protection for the group and for the special needs you might have identified.

8

Facing Personal Attacks

AIM: to learn how to respond to
personal pressures in our lives

Focus on the Theme

Imagine you have a particular job to do and you are not enthusiastic about doing it. Are you very focused or easily distracted? Can you give some examples from your own life (or your family) of the kinds of things that side-track you when there is a difficult job to be done?

Read: Nehemiah chapter 6

Key Verses: Nehemiah 6:1–13

Outline:

1. Distraction from the Task (6:1–4)

2. A Challenge to His Reputation (6:5–9)

3. The Temptation to Compromise (6:10–14)

As if the opposition Nehemiah had already encountered was not enough, he still faced three further challenges.

1. Distraction from the Task (6:1–4)

By chapter 6 verse 1 the wall was all but completed, and we might think that the opposition would realize it had lost the day. But no, the opposition was there at the beginning in chapter 1, it was there halfway through chapter 4, and it is here in chapter 6. Opposition to God's work is not only inevitable, it is sustained. We will face it until we finally reach our home in heaven. The enemies were active when the wall began, when the wall was half completed, and as the wall was nearing its completion. But the attacks now took a more subtle and more difficult turn. They were concentrated around Nehemiah himself.

The first, couched initially in diplomatic terms, was an attempt by Sanballat to eliminate Nehemiah. A messenger arrived suggesting it was time for negotiations. "Come, let us meet together in one of the villages on the plain of Ono" (v. 2). Let's sit down and talk it through. This was nothing more than a subtle piece of smooth talking as Nehemiah notes: "They were scheming to harm me" (v. 2). The work was in its final stages, and Nehemiah knew that, apart from the wasted time in travelling to the plain of Ono, the greater danger was the obvious personal threat to which he would become vulnerable if he left his friends.

So, what was his response to this form of opposition? It was clear and unequivocal: "I am carrying on a great project and cannot go down. Why should the work stop while I leave it and go down to you?" (v. 3). Four times they sent the same message (v. 4): don't be small-minded Nehemiah, be reasonable. But he refused to budge. The overriding priority was the work God had called him to do, and he would not be distracted or diverted from it. That's a common form of attack for us Christians, isn't it? Satan often whispers, "You've done OK, you can relax a little. There's no need to be a fanatic." We are frequently tempted by diversions and distractions of all kinds.

Sometimes they can be entirely legitimate things, which mean that the priority calling is neglected. It happened in the early church. Luke records in Acts 6 how the apostles were confronted with a problem within the Christian community that not only had the potential to cause division but, equally seriously, was in danger of diverting them from their primary tasks. Wisely they called others to deal with the immediate practical problem so that they could give their attention to the ministry of the Word and prayer.

We need to learn from Nehemiah's response. In the face of distraction, remember your calling.

We Christians can sometimes suffer from divided loyalties. Can you think of some examples?

"I am carrying out a great project and cannot go down," said Nehemiah (v. 3). What would you define as the work God has called you to do from which you should not be distracted?

2. A Challenge to His Reputation (6:5–9)

Having failed to pull Nehemiah away from the work, Sanballat decided to turn the screw a little more. On the fifth attempt, Sanballat's aide arrived with an open letter. Let me paraphrase: "Rumour has it that you are actually planning an armed revolt against the Persian king and would like the throne for yourself. Would you care to comment?" (v. 6).

Being unsealed, of course, it was the equivalent to a letter to a national newspaper. It was a slanderous accusation, and it was now out in the open, outside Nehemiah's control. As we've seen, the king had earlier put a stop to the rebuilding programme that had been attempted (Ezra 4), precisely because of such an accusation. So Sanballat was adopting a smear campaign to blackmail Nehemiah. It is what in political jargon is called "opposition research." You try to manufacture something that will smear the character, some mud that might stick. The victim's only defence is a clear conscience. Nehemiah could reply with integrity, "Nothing like what you are saying is happening; you are just making it up out of your head" (v. 8).

The ability to live our lives with integrity is the only protection against that kind of slander. It is impressive that when Paul was criticized, he could frequently appeal to both fellow Christians and to God himself as a witness of how he had lived. "You are witnesses, and so is God, of how holy, righteous, and blameless we were among you who believed" (1 Thess 2:5, 10). Nehemiah and Paul knew that the best response, when their motives or character were attacked, was to keep a clear conscience. It will be painful when people say things about you that are not true. For this we need the Lord's help: "Now strengthen my hands" (v. 9). Ignore the gossip; trust your cause to God.

Maybe you know Christian brothers and sisters who are facing this kind of opposition, whose names are blackened and whose reputation is under pressure. Pray for them as a group and ask God to give them the strength to keep a clear conscience in the light of his Word.

3. The Temptation to Compromise (6:10–14)

The final attack was subtler still. Shemaiah informed Nehemiah that he was on a hit list: "By night they are coming to kill you" (v. 10). So he urged him to take refuge inside the temple. Coming from someone who professed to be a prophet, the proposal had a religious veneer. But Nehemiah was just as uncompromising as ever.

First, there was no way in which he would be seen to run. He would lose credibility as a leader if he tried to hide from threatened attack. But second, there was no way in which he would enter the temple (v. 12). He was a layman, not a priest, and he knew that to enter the temple, even under the excuse of saving his life, would only end in disaster. It was not permitted in the Scriptures. Because he knew God's Word, he could test the prophecy.

> "I realized that God had not sent him, but that he had prophesied against me because Tobiah and Sanballat had hired him. He had been hired to intimidate me so that I would commit a sin by doing this, and then they would give me a bad name to discredit me." (vv. 12, 13)

His response to this attack: he was determined to live by the truth. John Calvin said, "It is an artifice of Satan to seek some misconduct on the part of ministers which may tend to the dishonour of the gospel."[1]

It is not only Christian leaders but all of us who face such pressure. We are constantly tempted to compromise. It might be to compromise on the essential truth of the Christian faith. It might be the temptation to compromise on its moral demands on our lives. It might be the temptation to compromise sexually, or financially, or to misuse power. Our protection will be to live by the truth, for our lives to be shaped by that Word, and for the Spirit to empower us to be consistent in living by its standards.

---

1. John Calvin, *Calvin's Commentary on the Bible*, 2 Corinthians 6:7, 147.

What kind of potential compromise do you face? Are there situations at work where life would be easier if you didn't hold out for Christian values? Are there situations in the church where the dangers of compromise are especially evident?

John Stott once said that if Christians in the West compromised less, they would undoubtedly suffer more. As Dietrich Bonhoeffer wrote in *The Cost of Discipleship*, before he was executed by the direct orders of Himmler shortly before the Allies liberated the concentration camp in which he was being held, "Suffering, then, is the badge of the true Christian." There is no escaping it if we name the name of Christ.

But the story of Nehemiah chapters 4 and 6 highlights the twin themes with which we began this section – the progress of the boat as it beats against the winds. The winds kept on blowing for Nehemiah. In chapter 6 the account is punctuated three times by his diary note: "They were all trying to frighten us" (v. 9); "the prophets have been trying to intimidate me" (v. 14). Even after the wall was completed, the slander and intimidation kept coming: "And Tobiah sent letters to intimidate me" (v. 19). This is what Alec Motyer once called "the constant dripping of Satanic acid." Deceit, espionage, slander – something coming through the post every day to eat away at his morale and to distract him from the job God had called him to do.

But those winds had the opposite effect. They enabled Nehemiah and the people to finish the task because they focused their attention on what really mattered. They trusted God more wholeheartedly. It's when we're in this situation that God teaches us to hold him fast. The winds against us are the very things that help us to complete the journey. "When all our enemies heard about this, all the surrounding nations were afraid and lost their self-confidence, because they realized that this work had been done with the help of our God" (6:16).

We all need to have the assurance that it is the sovereign Lord, the God of heaven, who will fulfil his purposes with us and through us. Just as I learned the lesson sailing against the wind in Scotland, so God would say to all hard-pressed Christians that his purpose is not to bypass difficulties in our lives, but to transform them.

Further Study

Read Acts 6:1–7. Here's an example of leaders who were in danger of losing sight of their priorities. What principles can you draw from these verses with regard to overcoming distractions from our primary purpose?

Reflection and Response

Nehemiah chapters 4 and 6 have given us an overview of the many pressures that God's people face. They are powerful examples of faith in the face of danger. Try to identify which of the different forms of opposition are especially significant at this time – for you or for your church – and make this a matter of focused prayer and action.

Review of Section 3: Nehemiah 4 and 6

This section of Nehemiah has touched on some demanding themes that relate very directly to Christian discipleship – to the challenges of spiritual life, spiritual warfare, and spiritual growth. It is especially important to spend time praying for the Lord's protection, both for yourself, your small group, and your church.

As we have seen, the forms of attack on Christian disciples come in various shapes and sizes, some direct and hostile and some subtle and persuasive. Share with a good friend the kind of pressures you face in your Christian life, and pray together for the Lord's protection. Leaders are also vulnerable: pray for those with pastoral and leadership responsibility in your church.

Remember the resources to which we have referred in Ephesians 6:10–19.

Section 4

Responding to God's Word

Nehemiah 8 and 9

Responding to God's Word

Introduction to Section 4

"I believe in a bit of everything – God, the supernatural, ghosts, superstitions, UFOs. I like to keep my options open." These words, of the former England cricket captain Mike Gatting, sum up the extraordinary sense of confusion that characterizes people's beliefs today. They illustrate that "when people stop believing in the truth, they don't believe in nothing, they believe in anything."

In many parts of the world, people seem to be turning away from traditional forms of faith, associated with a dogmatic approach, and instead they are looking for a more experiential faith. There are now several common views, from the more traditional to the more popular. The traditional view is that truth is objective, independent of the mind of the knower. It's there to be discovered. A more common view today is shaped by relativism – truth "as each person sees it." According to this view, truth is one thing to you and another thing to me. Then there is the post-modern perspective in which truth is not there to be discovered, but it is for "each of us to create for ourselves" – the truth is what I make it. Perhaps in some of our countries we have also entered the era of "post-truth," where there is less and less commitment to the idea of any agreed upon body of facts.

Increasingly people think that truth is entirely subjective. It's true because I like it; it's true if it helps me. Truth is a commodity to be moulded to serve my needs. When a Christian student who was having some struggles went to a university counsellor, she was advised to go and sleep with her boyfriend. "No, I'm a Christian, that's wrong," she replied. The student counsellor responded, "If it's functionally helpful, then it's legitimate." This is truth that is shaped according to the patterns of our own desires and convenience; truth that makes no demands on us. If it helps, then it must be true. The inevitable result of this view is that ultimately people – and societies – lose their bearings, becoming confused and morally bewildered.

It would be easy for Christians to respond with a degree of I-told-you-so smugness, or with much wringing of hands. But we must feel our responsibility for the situation and, like Nehemiah, we should resist the temptation to stand apart, indifferent to the moral and spiritual decline, and see that God has called us to serve him at a unique moment. If it is true that many people have an underlying longing for some form of spirituality, then this is also a hopeful moment. As God's people, we have the opportunity to try to respond to today's bewilderment and uncertainty.

In Nehemiah 8 we encounter an extraordinary turning point in the reconstruction of the national life of God's people. The rebuilding of the wall was finished, but that represented only the beginning. What really mattered was the shaping of the people, the reordering of their community life according to a solid constitution, with a proper foundation for their future as the distinct people of a holy God.

> When the seventh month came and the Israelites had settled in their towns, all the people assembled as one in the square before the Water Gate. They told Ezra the teacher of the Law to bring out the Book of the Law of Moses, which the LORD had commanded for Israel. (8:1)

They were about to embark on a massive re-education programme, which was to form the foundation for their spiritual, moral, social and economic life. As Derek Kidner says, they were to become "the people of the Book."[1]

Would it be an exaggeration to say that today, as God's people, we too need to engage in a massive programme of re-education? If God's Word were more fully a part of our lives, transforming us in our families, our worship, our professional life, and our social and moral behaviour, we would be living as people of hope in a despairing society.

Those who comment on the state of the church today suggest that we too have drifted. Writing some forty years ago in his book, *God Has Spoken*, Jim Packer said:

> At no time, perhaps, since the Reformation have Protestant Christians, as a body, been so unsure, tentative and confused as to what they should believe and do. Certainty about the great issues of Christian faith and conduct is lacking all along the line. The outside observer sees us staggering on from gimmick to gimmick and stunt to stunt like so many drunks in a fog, not knowing at all where we are or which way we should be going. Preaching is

---

1. Derek Kidner, *Ezra and Nehemiah*, Tyndale Old Testament Commentary (Leicester: IVP, 1979), 106.

hazy; heads are muddled; hearts fret; doubts drain our strength; uncertainty paralyses action.[2]

Since Dr Packer wrote those words, maybe there are signs of a turning of the tide. Christian people are longing to live lives that reflect God's standards, to do more than accumulate scriptural knowledge, and to experience the transforming power of that Word. But for sure, there is a long way to go. There is therefore much to be learned from the next section of Nehemiah's story.

---

2. J. I. Packer, *God Has Spoken* (London: Hodder & Stoughton, 1979), 20.

9

The Foundation of God's Word

AIM: to see why God's Word must be central to our lives and churches

Focus on the Theme

We all know that the Bible is a best-seller worldwide. But like Stephen Hawking's *A Brief History of Time*, it tends to sit unopened on shelves and coffee tables. Discuss together why you think the Bible is one of the most bought yet least read books?

Read: Nehemiah chapter 8

Key Verses: Nehemiah 8:1–12

Outline:

1. Its Centrality

2. Its Authority

3. Its Accessibility

Nehemiah 8 introduces us to something with which many of us are familiar: a seven-day Bible conference. It marks the close of the narrative we have been following thus far and introduces us to a new section of the book with three vital chapters all about the spiritual restoration of God's people, under the shared leadership of Ezra and Nehemiah.

It's possible that this section of Nehemiah once belonged between Ezra 8 and 9. But its place here, at the centre of Nehemiah's account, is theologically significant. The building of the walls might be over, but the true foundation for the restored community will be God's Word. Nehemiah knew how central and strategic this would be, and so he ensures that Ezra, the scholar-teacher, now comes to the forefront.

I suggest three features of the text that demonstrate that Ezra and Nehemiah saw the Word of God as the foundation for all that was to follow:

1. Its Centrality

The seventh month for God's people was a month of great religious festivity, and their first act was to call for the Book. There was a grassroots desire that the Law should be read: "All the people came together as one in the square before the Water Gate. They told Ezra the teacher of the Law to bring out the Book of the Law of Moses, which the LORD had commanded for Israel" (8:1), and the Law commanded the attention of everyone: "all the people listened attentively" (v. 3); "On the second day of the month, the heads of all the families . . . gathered round Ezra the teacher of the Law to give attention to the words of the Law" (v. 13); "Day after day, from the first day to the last, Ezra read from the Book of the Law of God" (v. 18).

It retained its central place right through to the end of the month: "They stood where they were and read from the Book of the Law of the LORD their God for a quarter of the day" (9:3). At the end of chapter 12, we have the account of the joyful processions as the walls are dedicated, and Nehemiah records, "On that day the Book of Moses was read aloud in the hearing of the people" (13:1). The Word of God represented the foundation articles, the new constitution for the people of God. They had returned from exile to Jerusalem and now, placed at the very centre of their life, was the Book of the Law that the Lord had provided for them. It defined their identity.

In the Central Asian Republics, children now have to learn huge chunks of the Qu'ran in their Islamic schools. Stalin may have closed twenty-six thousand mosques, but new investment is ensuring that the book is being read as a foundation for Islam in the battle of ideologies in this post-Soviet world. What about the place of the Book, God's Word, in our own society? We may now be in a post-Christian culture, but one of our challenges is to call people back to Scripture. When Theodore Roosevelt wrote about Abraham Lincoln, he described his core commitments: "Lincoln built up his entire reading upon his study of the Bible. He mastered it and became a man who knew the Book and instinctively put into practice what he had been taught therein."[1]

That was the desire of the Jews on that day recorded in Nehemiah 8:1. For a nation seeking its identity and shaping its programme of restoration, the Word of God mattered. It was central. There is even something symbolic in the fact that it was not read in the temple: "He read it aloud from daybreak till noon as he faced the square before the Water Gate" (v. 3). It was read "at one of the centres of city life, the kind of place where God's wisdom needs most urgently to be heard. The law itself insisted that its voice must not be confined to the sanctuary but heard in the house and the street."[2]

This is stressed in Deuteronomy 6:7, "Impress them on your children. Talk about them when you sit at home and when you walk along the road." Make the truth of God's Word central to the whole of life.

Do you think the Bible has a central place in your church? What kinds of things displace the Bible, nudging it to the periphery of our lives and Christian community?

What do you find is most helpful to you in reading the Bible regularly? We all need help here, so share as many practical ideas as you can.

---

2. Its Authority

> They told Ezra the teacher of the Law to bring out the Book of the
> Law of Moses, which the LORD had commanded for Israel. (v. 1)

Its human authorship is acknowledged on several occasions – the reading was from the books of Moses. But here its divine authority is also emphasized – it is the Law of God, the revelation given by him. The instruction came from God himself for their well-being. We are sometimes accused as evangelicals of just venerating an ancient text, and without this sense of divine authority that might be true. But the Bible is truly the word God has spoken, and it is

---

1. Theodore Roosevelt in *Lincoln's Use of the Bible* by Samuel Trevena Jackson, The Library of Alexandria.

2. Kidner, *Ezra and Nehemiah*, 105.

vital we realize that this word has authority precisely because of the one who speaks that word.

There is a significant explanation of this theme in 1 Thessalonians 2:13, where Paul describes the way in which the believers received the gospel. It is a key explanation of apostolic authority that can transform our attitude to the Bible. "We also thank God continually because, when you received the word of God, which you heard from us, you accepted it not as a human word, but as it actually is, the word of God, which is indeed at work in you who believe."

Note four implications:

Its authority: It is "the Word of God." Paul writes emphatically that the message of the apostles is authoritative because it originates with God himself. There is no doubt that in our pluralistic culture we need to preach the Word with great sensitivity and humility. But we should acknowledge that this is the Word of God and, like the early Christians, we should therefore proclaim it with boldness. We are often tempted to lose our nerve in affirming Jesus as the only way and the Scriptures as the Word of God, but Paul is adamant that the message has divine authority. It is the absolute truth for all cultures and every generation.

Its power: ". . . which is indeed at work in you who believe." It is powerful precisely because it is God's Word. We shouldn't drive a wedge between the written Word and the living God who speaks that word. By God's Spirit it is powerful, life-giving, life-transforming. You could translate the verse, "It goes on working in those who go on believing."

Its reception: Paul thanks God that the Thessalonian believers "accepted it" as God's Word. He uses two words in verse 13 – they "received" the Word (they heard it), but they also "accepted" it; they welcomed it in as a friend, it became part of them, continuing its work in their lives.

Its impact: In 1 Thessalonians 1:8–9 he describes the way in which they turned from idols to serve the living God. Then, "the Lord's message rang out from you . . . your faith in God has become known everywhere."

God's transforming Word is not simply propositional truth, cold and remote, but a dynamic Word that, by the power of the Spirit, turns us round to serve God and shapes the way we live. That same dynamic of God's Word was operating in Jerusalem as the Law was read to the assembled crowd.

Can you give an example of how God's Word has been at work in your life or in your church? In what ways has its authority and power been demonstrated?

3. Its Accessibility

If God's Word was to be the foundation for families' day-to-day living, society and relationships, then it had to be clear and accessible to everyone. There are two features to notice.

First, everyone was present. "All the people came together as one" (8:1); Ezra read before the assembly, verse 2, "which was made up of men and women and all who were able to understand" (children); then verse 5, "all the people could see him" (no TV monitors but a wooden tower); verse 9, "all the people had been weeping"; verse 13, "the heads of all the families."

Every attempt was made to ensure that everyone was present. Verse 4 demonstrates that Ezra gathered a team together to help with the reading. It was not just for priests or Levites, the religious professionals, but for all, and it was read, not in the religious building (the temple), but in the city centre, in the square in front of the Water Gate (v. 1).

It was not only vital that everyone was present. Second, everyone understood. The account shows us the stress placed on understanding for men, women, and children (v. 2). The content of the law had to be clear, "giving the meaning so that the people understood what was being read" (v. 8). The reason for the people's response therefore follows: "because they now understood the words that had been made known to them" (v. 12).

It is possible that the Levites in verses 7 and 8 were involved in translation into the language that the people understood – Aramaic and various dialects. Or, it's possible that they moved through the crowds holding small group Bible studies, explaining what the text meant.

What comes across clearly is the need to make the Book accessible to everybody, whether in the manner in which Ezra used his team or the location he chose for the reading or the tower that was constructed or the groups of translators and expositors and Bible study group leaders that he employed.

We need hardly make the point of application about the foundation of God's Word. We need to work creatively today to ensure that everyone is exposed to the truth of Scripture through sustaining clear, relevant, applied Bible exposition but also through the many interactive approaches, through small groups, personal study, and through new media that are now available to us.

It is God's authoritative, powerful, and life-transforming Word. It is the foundation for our lives and for our Christian community, and it is a Word for our world.

Discuss ways in which we can help children gain an excitement for the Bible. How can we help them read, understand, and love God's Word?

Share some ways in which we can make the Bible more central in our homes. Most of us find it very difficult to use the Bible in a family context: can you encourage one another with some practical ideas?

Are there ways of helping to make the Bible more central and accessible in the church? What can we do to encourage more public reading, more obvious ways of signalling its importance, and more ways of exposing a wider cross-section of people to its powerful influence?

Further Study

There are some powerful illustrations of the dynamic of God's Word in the following passages. How do they strengthen our understanding of the ways in which the Bible works in our lives?

Psalm 33:4–9

Psalm 119:11, 89, 105, 130

Isaiah 55:11

Jeremiah 23:29

Luke 8:1–15

John 8:32

Acts 12:24

Ephesians 6:17

Colossians 3:16

2 Timothy 2:9

Hebrews 4:12, 13

James 1:18

1 Peter 1:23–25

1 John 2:14

Reflection and Response

Given the availability of translations, reading guides, study resources, and daily reading plans, what practical steps can you take as a group to encourage one another to enjoy the riches of the Bible on a daily basis?

10

The Hunger of God's People

AIM: to learn the prerequisites for experiencing God's blessing

Focus on the Theme

Describe your typical Sunday morning, from the ringing of the alarm clock to arriving at the church service.

Read: Nehemiah chapter 8

Key Verses: Nehemiah 8:9–18

Outline:

1. Their Expectancy

2. Their Commitment

3. Their Reverence

Having seen the central place that Ezra and Nehemiah gave to the reading of the Law, we now look at how the people responded as they heard the Word of the Lord. There are three themes to point out.

87

1. Their Expectancy

First, it is clear that they were eager to hear the Word. They wanted the Law and the Lord to speak to them. They took the initiative, calling on Ezra to bring out the Book. Jim Packer makes an intriguing comment: "Imagine an impatient audience at a rock concert picking up the chant, 'We want Ezra,' saying it over and over, louder and louder, and you get some idea of the feelings being expressed."[1]

The same sense of eagerness and expectancy is expressed in verse 3: "all the people listened attentively"; verse 5, as the people "stood up" when the Book was opened; and verse 13: everyone gathered "to give attention to the words of the Law."

It reminds us of Luke's comment in Acts 17:11 when he describes the Bereans, who "received the message with great eagerness and examined the Scriptures every day to see if what Paul said was true." It also reminds us that there is little to be gained from reading the Bible without such expectancy. Jesus's own ministry was frustrated when there was no expectancy on the part of some of his hearers. He began to teach in the synagogue, and he was met with cynicism and incredulity. Expectant faith is the soil in which God's Word will bear fruit in our lives.

Why do you think there is often so little expectancy when we come to God's Word – either in personal reading or when we gather as a church?

In what ways can that be changed?

---

2. Their Commitment

A further sign of their spiritual hunger was their seriousness. They were ready to cope with all kinds of inconvenience in order to hear this Word. I have sometimes been in Eastern European countries where, after preaching for an hour or more, the congregation wonders why you've stopped. Here the Water Gate congregation stood from daybreak to noon (v. 3) – for at least five hours, without a coffee-break in sight – because they longed to hear and understand what God had to say to them.

---

1. Packer, *Passion for Faithfulness*, 150.

Again, we have to conclude that such commitment to God's Word, and eagerness to hear from him, was to do with the work of God's Spirit. There are many things we need to do to make God's Word accessible and understandable, but more than anything else, we need the Holy Spirit to reverse the tide, to create within us and within our churches – and even in our society and among our politicians – a hunger for what God has to say to us.

All around the world there is evidence of a decline in personal and group Bible study. We ought to pray much, much more for this kind of expectancy and seriousness if we are going to reverse the decline. A Bible Society survey in my country showed that almost 40 percent of churchgoers read the Bible at home only once a year or less. It is a paradox in a country where the Scriptures are available in all kinds of translations and on many different electronic platforms. Sadly, similar problems exist in country after country around the world: more and more Christians have access to the Bible, yet too few of us take it seriously.

Our congregations will never mature, our impact on society will never be significant, and our hopes of revival will remain distant, until we develop a stronger desire to read, understand and apply this living dynamic Word to our lives. This is what the weekly preaching in our churches is all about: not just reading for its own sake, but opening God's Word so as to bring us into God's presence, transform our lives, and impact our society.

Are there ways in which your group can help each member recover the importance of commitment to Scripture?

---

3. Their Reverence

Ezra praised the LORD, the great God; and all the people lifted their hands and responded, "Amen! Amen!" Then they bowed down and worshipped the LORD with their faces to the ground. (v. 6)

Today, there is a right sense in which we are concerned to make our church events seeker-friendly and welcoming. We shouldn't have cultural barriers preventing people from attending, but along the way we might sometimes have lost a degree of reverence that is appropriate in worship.

I am not suggesting we must all adopt the custom of some churches, whereby the congregation stands as the Word of God is carried into the church.

But maybe there is something to learn from the attitude of the people in Jerusalem on that day – a longing for God to speak as they lifted up their hands, a self-abasement or reverence as they bowed with their faces to the ground.

Perhaps these too are prerequisites to understanding God's Word and coming into his presence. Indeed, the verse is important in reminding us that we don't venerate the Book as such. Its purpose is to bring us into the presence of the author, the Lord, the great God. Luther used to describe Scripture as "the cradle in which we will find the baby." Its purpose is not to draw attention to itself, but to introduce us to the person of Jesus. We come to Scripture because it is one of the primary ways by which the Spirit will lead us into his presence.

Because it is the dynamic, living Word, it will introduce us to the living God and transform us into his likeness. Jim Packer says in his book, *God Has Spoken*:

> The joy of Bible study is not the fun of collecting esoteric titbits about Gog and Magog, Tubal Cain and Methusalah, Bible numerics, and the beast, and so on; nor is it the pleasure, intense for the tidy minded, of analyzing our translated text into preachers' pretty patterns, with neatly numbered headings held together by apt alliterations' artful aid. Rather, it is the deep contentment that comes from communing with the living Lord into whose presence the Bible takes us – a joy that only his own true disciples know.[2]

Can you give examples of how you have encountered the Lord through the pages of Scripture?

What might it mean for your church to bring together both reverence and celebration?

Further Study

Reverence and awe are not common responses in our worship today. Read Hebrews 12:18–29. In the context of Hebrews 12 as a whole, what do you think verses 28 and 29 imply for our worship?

2. Packer, *God Has Spoken*, 10.

Reflection and Response

Luther implied Scripture's focus is Jesus himself. In what ways do you think that is true, and what do you think are the implications?

11

The Implications of God's Grace

AIM: to rejoice in the wideness of God's mercy

Focus on the Theme

With our different personalities and our different cultural backgrounds, we might have different views about "religious emotions." Discuss together what you think might be legitimate emotions to display in the context of worship.

Read: Nehemiah chapter 9

Key Verses: Nehemiah 9:5–37

Outline:

1. Celebration

2. Confession

3. Commitment

So far we have noted the centrality and significance of the Law and the extraordinary response of God's people. But this section of Nehemiah's memoirs also records the actions of the people as they came to see what that Word truly represented. "For all the people had been weeping as they listened to the words of the Law" (Neh 8:9).

Their first hearing of the Law provoked within the people a sense of contrition as they realized that their lives had failed to match up to God's standards. But intriguingly, Ezra and Nehemiah set that failure within the wider context of God's purposes for his people.

> This day is holy to the LORD your God. Do not mourn or weep. . . .
> Go and enjoy choice food and sweet drinks, and send some to
> those who have nothing prepared. This day is holy to our Lord.
> Do not grieve, for the joy of the LORD is your strength. (8:9–10)

Their first response was to accept joyfully all that God has done for them. It was a special day, a day to recall God's grace upon them as his own people.

1. Celebration

This was how they were to respond to God's grace and, with the encouragement of the leaders, the people went to celebrate, to eat and drink "with great joy" (8:12). After hours of standing, they must have headed off for the party with added zest. Now that they were finally back home in Jerusalem, they had come to realize, from all that had been read, that God's desire was to bless them: "They now understood the words that had been made known to them" (v. 12).

That was the reason why the "joy of the LORD" was their strength – the word means their "fortress," their "stronghold." It's the awareness that God has good purposes for us, that his Law is for our benefit, and that his actions of mercy and grace are for our well-being, our shalom. Full appreciation of that generates a deep sense of joy and thanksgiving in our lives. It is the opposite of the anxiety that is so characteristic of our culture.

The note of joy runs on into the next section too. On the second day (vv. 13–15) their Bible study leads them to the discovery of the Feast of Booths, a harvest festival when they especially remembered deliverance from Egypt and the long march to the promised land. So, just as it was written in Leviticus 23, they went out and built their shanty huts. For seven days they were not just celebrating the liberation of God's people from Egypt but also their own return from exile.

"The whole company that had returned from exile built temporary shelters and lived in them. From the days of Joshua son of Nun until that day, the Israelites had not celebrated it like this. And their joy was very great" (v. 17). Notice that it was inclusive: they cared for those who were without resources – another dimension of their community life that demonstrated compassion for those in need.

Believe it or not, joy should be the hallmark of true Christian faith. Of course, how we express it sometimes has to do with our personality or our culture, both of which God respects. But what have we done to provoke so many people to imagine that the Christian faith is quite the opposite of what is described here? Reverence and joy are not incompatible.

Before his conversion, Ernest Gordon, the author of *Miracle on the River Kwai*, thought of Christians as people who extracted the bubbles from the champagne of life. He said "I would prefer a robust hell to the grey, sunless abode of the faithful." I know that when people describe the church as deadly boring it is saying as much about them as about the church, and so often there is the missing dimension of celebration.

I like the remark of the German pastor and theologian, Helmut Thielicke, "Should we not see that lines of laughter about the eyes are just as much marks of faith as are lines of care and seriousness? Is it only earnestness that is baptized? A church is in a bad way when it has banished laughter from the sanctuary and leaves it to the cabaret."[1]

The joy of the Lord is our strength – not a superficial triumphalism, but the certainty that God has nothing but good purposes for us as his people. That's what came home to them as they celebrated God's grace back home in Jerusalem. It is this same inner conviction that will also help us to rise above all kinds of challenges. God's purposes of grace are overwhelming, and as these realities sink into our hearts and minds, so the joy of the Lord will become our fortress too.

Can you think of a Christian known to you who demonstrates this kind of joy, even in demanding circumstances?

When Peter and Paul talk about rejoicing in sufferings, what are they getting at?

---

2. Confession

After the celebrations surrounding the Feast of Booths, the people now gather (9:1), fasting and wearing sackcloth and having dust on their heads. It is now

---

1. Helmut Thielicke, *Encounter with Spurgeon* (Cambridge: Lutterworth Press, 1967), xxxviii.

three and a half weeks after the Water Gate convention, and a national day of repentance and recommitment has been called.

Verses 5 to 38 represent a prayer that was the centre of the occasion. Notice again that the confession, like the celebration, arose from the reading of God's Word. "They stood where they were and read from the Book of the Law of the LORD their God for a quarter of the day . . ." (v. 3).

The prayer is beautifully constructed so that once again the content of God's Word gives shape to the worship. There are many quotations from Exodus, Leviticus, and Deuteronomy as it recounts the story of Israel from creation (5, 6) to election (7, 8), redemption (9–12), covenant and law (13–15), grace (16–18), patient persistence (19–25) through to judgment and righteousness (26–31).

We see in Nehemiah 8 and 9 how the people were reawakened to a sense of their national identity and history. But it was much more than that. They had come to see that Yahweh was their God and they were his people. The Spirit was at work showing them the depth of God's grace in calling them. These chapters record what we can describe as national renewal or revival.

It would be true to say that chapter 9, while introduced as a confession of sin, is much more a confession of faith. The structure of the prayer demonstrates an oscillation from admission of their failure back to an acknowledgement of God's grace and mercy to them. It shows us the commitment of the covenant Lord, his persevering steadfast love. There is a statement of God's goodness, then of the people's failure, then of his unfailing mercy.

Notice some of the turning points in the prayer:

Verse 17: "But you are a forgiving God, gracious and compassionate."

Verse 19: "Because of your great compassion you did not abandon them in the wilderness."

Verse 27: "From heaven you heard them, and in your great compassion you gave them deliverers, who rescued them from the hand of their enemies."

Verse 28: "When they cried out to you again, you heard from heaven, and in your compassion you delivered them time after time."

Verse 31: "But in your great mercy you did not put an end to them or abandon them, for you are a gracious and merciful God. Now therefore, our God, the great God, mighty and awesome, who keeps his covenant of love, do not let all this hardship seem trifling in your eyes."

Notice the "But" – the wonderful reversal in each of the story lines. Despite the sinfulness, despite the rebellion that had brought them into exile in the first place, God says "But." Paul, in Romans 3:21, shows how the "But" is the turning point of the gospel. "But now apart from the law a righteousness of God has been made known . . . all are justified freely by his grace through the redemption that came by Christ Jesus." Aren't you grateful for the "But now" of the gospel?

One of my first attempts to witness to the gospel was as a fourteen-year-old, speaking hesitantly at the London Embankment Mission to a crowd of men who had come in off the streets. "It's OK for you," one man said, "but you don't know what I've done. God could never forgive me." An older and wiser Christian who was with me pointed him to Psalm 103:11–13: "For as high as the heavens are above the earth, so great is his love for those who fear him; as far as the east is from the west, so far has he removed our transgressions from us. As a father has compassion on his children, so the LORD has compassion on those who fear him."

No one is beyond God's reach; no one need fear that God's forgiveness through the work of Jesus Christ is unavailable to them.

Nehemiah's confession of faith in chapter 9 declares that we need not feel the debilitating and demoralizing impact of failure. "But in your great mercy you did not put an end to them or abandon them, for you are a gracious and merciful God" (v. 31). As we know from the New Testament, Jesus declares to us, by his word and his work, that our sin is forgiven, our guilt is taken away, our pardon is guaranteed. Forgiveness has the liberating effect of lifting the burden. "If we confess our sins, he is faithful and just to forgive us our sins and purify us from all unrighteousness" (1 John 1:9).

Past failures need not hold us back. We sometimes behave as if we have a video of past failure, and even though God assures us it is forgiven and forgotten, we sit there rewinding the video – stop, rewind, play, stop, rewind, play. But our sin is "covered," as Psalm 51 declares. God's loving purpose for us is that we put down the remote control. We must let go of the past because he has done so, and we learn by his grace to accept the complete forgiveness he has provided in Christ and his cross. That is what the people in this passage recognized, this wonderful confession of faith: God, in his mercy, will not let go of us.

It is said that there is less and less emphasis on repentance today. Why do you think that is? What are the likely results if it is true?

How can confession during church prayer times be truly helpful, as opposed to a formal ritual?

Why do we sometimes find it hard to believe that we have been forgiven? What can make the difference in assuring us that it is true?

3. Commitment

The final response naturally follows. All who have experienced the restoring grace of God in their lives will want to commit themselves to live for him more and more fully, and so we see that the prayer moves the people towards a statement of covenant renewal. "In view of all this, we are making a binding agreement, putting it in writing, and our leaders, our Levites and our priests are affixing their seals to it" (v. 38).

They were going to obey God's Word. They were "binding themselves with a curse and an oath to follow the Law of God given through Moses the servant of God and to obey carefully all the commands, regulations, and decrees of the LORD our God" (10:29). They were ready for action. They wanted to live their lives in conformity with God's Word, to demonstrate in their community that they belonged to him.

That's the significance of the sequence of these chapters: it is hearing God's Word, celebrating God's goodness, knowing God's grace, and then obeying God's laws.

We are called to do the truth, not simply to believe it. That's the purpose of coming to the Book: to lead to determined faithfulness, to a change of lifestyle. The test of the value of Bible teaching is not so much whether we are stirred emotionally, but whether, as a result of our exposure to God's Word, we become more obedient.

If we're concerned about the welfare of our families and our children, if we are concerned about the moral and spiritual well-being of our nations, and if we are determined to play our part in God's purposes of restoration, then we must be people ready to respond to God's Word, committed to live the truth.

As the American evangelist D. L. Moody used to say, "Every Bible needs to be bound with shoe leather."

Further Study

Spend some time working through each paragraph of the remarkable prayer of Nehemiah 9. Try to summarize each section with one sentence that captures the attitude of the people and the Lord's response. Write out the specific encouragements from this prayer that you can take to heart in your own life.

Reflection and Response

Chapters 8 and 9 have focused on the renewal of God's people as they returned to Jerusalem. Getting back to their roots, they renewed their commitment to the Lord. Review these two chapters, listing the main foundations for the Christian life of which you have been reminded. How have these foundations helped you in your own Christian walk, and how can you keep them central?

Review of Section 4: Nehemiah 8 and 9

These chapters represent the heart of Nehemiah's memoirs, as the people confirm their commitment to the Lord and express their willingness to obey his commands. It is a good moment now to pause and to ask God to help you to respond to him as the people did in Jerusalem – hearing his Word, celebrating his grace and obeying his commands.

If it would help you, try to write a simple statement – a prayer – that represents your commitment to serve and obey the Lord.

Read the prayer of chapter 9 once again, taking note of the way in which God's grace and mercy are continually affirmed despite the rebellion of people like us. Spend some time in personal and group prayer as you ask God to strengthen your desire to read, understand, and obey his Word.

Section 5

Living by God's Standards

Nehemiah 10 and 13

Living by God's Standards

Introduction to Section 5

I once read a small item of news that surprisingly hit the international papers. It was the rather distressing story of a lorry driver who lost his job. The reason? Because he drove supply lorries for Coca Cola, and insisted on drinking cans of Pepsi at work. So he was fired.

A little unjust, you might think. Of course, if it had been the chief executive caught with a six-pack of Pepsi under his desk, that's another matter. Because these days, in the new styles of business management, consistency matters. Charles Handy, the business guru, lists as one of his six guiding principles for managers: "The leader must live the vision." He must not only craft his mission or vision statement; he must embody it. We feel the same about politicians. We're suspicious of manifesto pledges and political programmes at the best of times, but when there is no genuine change in the real world, we become cynical about the entire process. Many politicians are undermined by the public's perception of spin, or corruption, or a lack of integrity.

Christians in the first century couldn't afford inconsistency. As we read the New Testament, we see the close connection between holiness and mission. The early church was being watched; their lives, their work, their families, their values, their response under pressure – all of these had to support their radical message. This is effectively what John wrote: "Whoever claims to live in him must live as Jesus did" (1 John 2:6). It is a matter of faith that works, godliness in working clothes.

In fact, as we look at the biblical story, this was nothing new for those who were called to be God's people. It was a major Old Testament theme, and as we come to the closing chapters of the book of Nehemiah, we see that at the heart of the process of the rebuilding of God's people, there lay a concern for absolute consistency. God's people were to live by God's standards.

In this regard their uniqueness as a community – their distinct morality, social and economic relationships, and lifestyle – was to be a witness to the character of the God whom they worshipped. We have already touched on this theme in Nehemiah 5, but now in chapter 10, we come to the special agreement made by the people, the renewal of the covenant relationship, in which they affirm their "distinctness."

> The rest of the people – priests, Levites, gatekeepers, musicians, temple servants, and all who separated themselves from the neighbouring peoples for the sake of the Law of God, together with their wives and all their sons and daughters who are able to understand – all these now join their fellow Israelites the nobles, and bind themselves with a curse and an oath to follow the Law of God given through Moses the servant of God and to obey carefully all the commands, regulations, and decrees of the LORD our God. (10:28–29)

It is a misunderstanding to think that being "separated from the peoples" suggests an elitist or exclusivist mentality. The separation being spoken about was a religious separation. The peoples of neighbouring lands worshipped other gods, and so the call to be separate and distinct came from the first commandment: "You shall have no other gods before me." It was a declaration of their allegiance to Yahweh. They were following his Word, as Nehemiah 10 demonstrates: "all those who had separated themselves . . . for the sake of the Law of God" (10:28).

The way in which they lived would demonstrate their commitment to that one Lord and would be a witness to their neighbours of what the true God was like.

Belief matched by behaviour is as critical for effective mission today as it was then. I recently spoke with a colleague in East Asia who commented on the high percentage of Christians in Hong Kong. Among the university students, up to one-third are believers, yet they make so little difference in their society, he said. In the medical faculty, nearly 60 percent of the students are Christians. Yet they still work their tax dodges just like anyone else. The numbers of Christians might seem an encouragement, but what about their genuine Christian distinctness? We know this to be true in so many countries, and in our own lives too.

It is good to confront the challenges of chapter 10 and 13, where the people declare their commitment to God's standards, but where we subsequently find promise without performance.

The next chapter in this study guide will introduce the three themes which appear in Nehemiah 10. But since these three themes are picked up again in detail in Nehemiah 13, some of the questions and ideas for group discussion will be postponed until we come to the final chapter in this book.

12

Commitment to God's Standards

AIM: to learn what faithful obedience to God will mean

Focus on the Theme

Think about times when you have had to sign agreements and be held accountable? Can you explain why that is sometimes difficult?

Read: Nehemiah chapter 10

Key Verses: Nehemiah 9:38; 10:28–39

Outline:

1. The Identity of God's People
2. The Significance of God's Covenant
3. The Priority of God's House

As we have seen, in response to the reading of God's Word, the people make a solemn undertaking to live according to God's laws. They made a number of specific resolutions to be faithful (10:28–39). We will examine three and then in the next chapter take more time to look at the practical implications of living by such standards.

1. The Identity of God's People

> "We promise not to give our daughters in marriage to the peoples
> around us or take their daughters for our sons." (10:30)

When the "urge to merge" is a universal phenomenon, why do the people
support a restriction? As we've seen, the kind of separation being called for
was for religious not for racial reasons. The Old Testament law made it clear:
you can't possibly have a strong marriage if husband and wife are worshipping
different gods. Compromise would be inevitable for the follower of Yahweh,
who makes exclusive claims on his people.

Malachi used strong idiomatic language to condemn this kind of behaviour:
"Judah has desecrated the sanctuary the LORD loves by marrying women who
worship a foreign god" (Mal 2:11). He wasn't making a point about race or
ethnicity, but about true spiritual loyalty. He was deeply concerned to sustain
the identity of God's people, around whom God's purposes of redemption
were focused. This kind of inter-marriage would lead to a loss of faithfulness
to the one Lord, and a gradual erosion of the uniqueness of God's people.
Compromise would have disastrous consequences.

The people affirmed that they would live by God's standards. "We promise
not to give our daughters in marriage to the peoples around us . . ." (v. 30).

Look at the groups who signed up to the agreement (vv. 28–29). Why
do you think it was important that, after the reading of the law in chapter
8, and the response in chapter 9, they had to sign the agreement here
in chapter 10?

We will turn to the specifics of marriage relationships in the next chapter,
but can you identify areas in the life of the church where compromise
can weaken our sense of identity as God's people, and betray our
Christian witness?

---

2. The Significance of God's Covenant

> When the neighbouring peoples bring merchandise or grain to
> sell on the Sabbath, we will not buy from them on the Sabbath
> or on any holy day. Every seventh year we will forgo working the
> land and will cancel all debts. (10:31)

The Old Testament law had established several vital reasons why observing the Sabbath was at the heart of their distinctness as a nation. As a day of rest, it reflected the pattern of God's work and rest in creation, and it was also a time set aside for people to reflect on God's goodness and to worship him. It was a day when they acknowledged that God could continue to provide for their needs, even when they were not working, and was therefore a declaration of their allegiance to the Lord and their trust in his covenant promises to be faithful in his care for them. The temptation now, in Jerusalem, was to soft-pedal that idea.

Again, it's important to remember the circumstances. The exiles had come back to a gloomy situation. There was a huge amount to be done in the fields, many had not yet returned, much of the land was occupied by others, and the economy was struggling. There were foreign traders ready and willing to develop their market, even on the Sabbath. But on that day of national rededication, moved by God's Word and God's Spirit, the people were determined to express their loyalty to the teaching on the Sabbath. They would trust him fully to care for them.

Again, we will look at the specific issue of the Sabbath in the next chapter. But there is a basic principle we need to reflect on. Most of us live in a context where our daily food is provided and our normal human needs are cared for. Is there a danger that we might lose sight of our dependence on God? How can we cultivate a daily trust in the Lord for his provision?

The people in Jerusalem might have been tempted to take short cuts, rather than follow the Lord's instruction about trading on the Sabbath. In our Christian lives, are there temptations to side-step God's standards for the sake of convenience?

---

3. The Priority of God's House

The rest of chapter 10:32–39 is a statement of the people's commitment to the upkeep of the temple. Again, this goes back to many references to the Law (Exod 30), and the people now recognized their individual responsibility to give annually to sustain the ministry of the temple, which was right at the heart of the city, and represented their relationship with God himself.

That's why they had worked so hard to rebuild the city and restore the temple; this was the place where God was to be worshipped; this was to be their number one priority. They were to give: money (v. 32), grain (v. 33), wood for the altar (v. 34), first fruits of their crops (v. 35), and tithes (vv. 37–39) to support the priests and the Levites. "We will not neglect the house of our God," they said, knowing that if the temple went down, so would their relationship with God. Their commitment was substantial. It involved every family, it impacted their day-to-day lives, and it was a continuing obligation to acknowledge that everything they had belonged to God. Giving the first fruits of their crops declared that this was their first priority, the first call on their resources.

In summary, their agreement in chapter 10 struck at the heart of what it meant to be God's people: a distinct, holy nation, committed to the one God, trusting his faithfulness for every aspect of life. They were going to obey him at all costs and trust him to keep "his covenant of love." But that is not what happened. The next chapter will show us that, despite the promise, there was no performance.

If your group or church had to make a list of material things that were to be committed to the Lord, what would you include?

Further Study

After talking about what you should eat and what you should wear, Jesus said, "But seek first God's kingdom and righteousness, and all these things will be given you as well" (Matt 6:33). What did he mean in terms of Christian priorities? Can you think of practical examples of how the principle Jesus gives us is seen to work?

Reflection and Response

Perhaps the most common criticism of Christians is their capacity to be hypocrites. In what ways are you in danger of "play-acting"? In what ways does your attitude or behaviour fail to match your professed belief? Spend some time in confession and prayer as you ask for God's help to live a consistent life.

13

Promise without Performance

AIM: to understand the importance of obedience in living lives of integrity

Focus on the Theme

Can you think of times when someone has made a promise to you and has failed to keep it? How did you feel? Can you share examples of times when you have made a promise or commitment to the Lord and have failed to keep it? How might he feel?

Read: Nehemiah chapter 13

Key Verses: Nehemiah 13:6–27

Outline:

1. The Priority of God's House – and the Result of Indifference
2. The Significance of God's Covenant – and the Drift towards Expediency
3. The Identity of God's People – and the Danger of Compromise

Trying to live lives of committed Christian discipleship in today's world demands constant vigilance, constant dependence on the power of God's Word and Spirit. We face the daily pressure to conform to the world's standards, the subtle and insidious influence of secularism. We hardly notice the drift away from God's standards, the dilution of our committed resolve to be followers of Jesus Christ.

As God's people, we gradually lose our distinctness, and it was no different in Nehemiah's day: that is exactly the situation he encountered towards the end of his leadership in Jerusalem. After his first term as governor, Nehemiah had returned to Susa to fulfil his responsibilities for King Artaxerxes. When he came back to Jerusalem for a second term as governor, about twenty years after the people had made their solemn commitments in chapter 10, he would have been around sixty-five years old. But instead of coming home to retire, Nehemiah discovered that his work was not over. His motto must have been, "I've started, so I'll finish."

By chapter 13, we discover that a terrible spiritual decline had set in. Far from sustaining their distinctness as God's people, they had drifted away from God's standards. After all of the promises, there was no performance. After the incredible feat of rebuilding the wall, after revival in the city at the reading of God's Word, after the solemn and binding commitments made by the people in the service of covenant renewal, Nehemiah returns to discover a self-serving bunch of individualists, not the dedicated people of God. We are given a very realistic view of what can happen and a very human insight into the struggles Nehemiah faced in urging the people to remain faithful.

Many contemporary expressions of Christian hope for revival imagine that it will be instantaneous – that God will change me, the church, and society as if by a magic wand. But there are no buttons to press for automatic renewal in the Christian life. There might be a tendency in contemporary evangelicalism to be attracted to apparently quick-fix solutions to our corporate problems, miraculous interventions or slick strategies that will deliver growth and renewal, but there are no such instant solutions. There is instead what one writer has called "a long obedience in the same direction" – a firm and disciplined commitment to trust God's Word, depend on God's Spirit, and live in God's community. Otherwise there will be drift towards compromise and decay.

What did Nehemiah discover on his return to Jerusalem? We will look at exactly the same three themes that we examined in the previous chapter, but in reverse order.

1. The Priority of God's House – and the Result of Indifference

Verses 4–9 reintroduce us to Nehemiah's old enemy, Tobiah, whom we saw in chapters 4 and 6. With good social and political connections in the city, he had by now infiltrated to such an extent that even the high priest Eliashib had offered him favours. "He had provided him with a large room formerly used to store the grain offerings and incense and temple articles, and also the tithes of grain, new wine, and olive oil prescribed for the Levites, musicians, and gatekeepers, as well as the contributions for the priests" (v. 5).

When Nehemiah discovered this, he was furious. Apart from the strategic danger from this kind of insidious infiltration, Tobiah was a layman and had no right to be in the temple. Taking over the storeroom had resulted in ceremonial defilement.

Behind this incident was another serious issue. Eliashib had apparently been happy to give Tobiah the temple room because it wasn't needed for its purpose of storage – tithing had gradually declined, and as Nehemiah recorded, "I also learned that the portions assigned to the Levites had not been given to them, and that all the Levites and musicians responsible for the service had gone back to their own fields" (v. 10). The Levites depended on the gifts for their income, and now these had dried up, they had to go out and work the fields. The temple services were being neglected.

Acting decisively, Nehemiah says, "I was greatly displeased and threw all Tobiah's household goods out of the room. I gave orders to purify the rooms, and then I put back into them the equipment of the house of God, with the grain offerings and the incense" (v. 8).

It's a reminder of Jesus's own determination to honour God's house when he made a whip and drove out the money changers from the temple area. "Get out of here! Stop turning my Father's house into a market!" (John 2:16). That was also Nehemiah's passion: "So I rebuked the officials and asked them, 'Why is the house of God neglected?'" (v. 11).

Do you remember the last verse of chapter 10? "We will not neglect the house of our God." But it was promise without performance. They had become indifferent to the priority of God's house. So Nehemiah appointed trustworthy men to be in charge of the storerooms (v. 13), to ensure that the pledges made twenty years earlier were going to be fulfilled.

Of course, our situation is very different from the fifth century BC. But the New Testament teaches us that both the Christian and the church are God's temple, indwelt by the Spirit, and it is all too easy for there to be defilement right at the heart of that temple. "Besetting sins, unhallowed relationships, the self-serving pursuit of pleasure, profit, power, or position, unconcern about pleasing and glorifying God, and any pattern of action that in any way undermines obedience to God's written Word and fidelity to the Christ of the Scriptures has a defiling effect in God's sight," says Jim Packer.[1] If that is something we have come to realize in our lives or in our churches, then Nehemiah's action is also an example for us: remove the bad, restore the good.

One of the main lessons of this chapter is that we need to watch out for those things that can produce an indifference to God's cause. We can so easily be affected by the materialism of our day, where personal wealth displaces the things of God. We neglect the priority of God's work in some way, and that is soon exploited by a Tobiah, who secures his toehold and begins the process of defilement.

Given the strong statements the people made in the covenant agreement of chapter 10, how do you think they could have gone this far astray in chapter 13?

What are the influences in our lives that will lead to similar indifference, and how can we avoid such a drift?

---

2. The Significance of God's Covenant – and the Drift towards Expediency

Verses 15–22 describe the next disappointment for Nehemiah. We have seen from chapter 10 why the command to honour the Sabbath regulations was a significant call to God's people to remain distinct, to be God's covenant community. Nehemiah had urged a rigorous enforcement of that law. And what did he find twenty years later?

"In those days I saw people in Judah treading winepresses on the Sabbath and bringing in grain and loading it on donkeys, together with wine, grapes, figs and all other kinds of loads. And they were bringing all this into Jerusalem on the Sabbath" (v. 15). In verse 16, Phoenician merchants were setting up their stalls at the Fish Gate and trading on the Sabbath. As the people became indifferent to God's house, they had also turned their backs on their earlier commitment to the Sabbath by a drift towards commercial expediency. When Gentile traders arrived in Jerusalem, they found nothing distinct about the nation, no devotion or loyalty on the part of the so-called people of God.

---

1. Packer, *Passion for Faithfulness*, 188.

Again, Nehemiah rebukes the leaders in Jerusalem: "What is this wicked thing you are doing – desecrating the Sabbath day?" (v. 17). He warns them of the potentially disastrous consequences. It was precisely because of their forefathers' failure to honour the covenant that Jerusalem had been destroyed by the Babylonians and the people had been carted off into exile. History was in danger of repeating itself.

Nehemiah's determined action (vv. 19–21) shows a man who is totally committed to sustaining God's standards, who refuses to accept a drift towards an easy religion where faith is shaped by personal expediency rather than godly determination. Nehemiah saw that the decision to ignore the Sabbath was a denial of faith in God.

Again, what are we to make of this in the twenty-first century? Much has been written about the way Christians view the Sabbath, or how they should treat Sunday. What is clear from Scripture, as a whole, is that this special day is an important paradigm for Christians. Both creation and redemption remind us of its importance. As a creation ordinance, we see it as part of the rhythm of our lives when God has made us rest from our usual labours. But if we fail to take the creation ordinance seriously, we will find it will impact our whole lives. This is coupled with the importance of the Lord's Day as the day of spiritual refreshment and renewal, the day for honouring and worshipping God with a distinctness that marks us out as his people. We are not under Old Testament Sabbath laws and we should not be put off by what we sometimes call the neo-Sabbatarians who try to import much of the old covenant into the new.

However, that does not mean that the Lord's Day has no significance for Christians. It is not easy to balance all the demands of life in our society, but we need to find ways of ensuring that we affirm that the Son of Man is Lord of the Sabbath. That includes the essential priority of worship with God's people and the importance of spiritual renewal. The Puritan Thomas Watson wrote, "When the falling dust of the world has clogged the wheels of our affections so that they can scarcely move towards God, the Sabbath/Sunday comes and oils the wheels of our own affections and they move swiftly on."[2]

Actually, Sundays can be very busy days for many of us. We live as though Jesus had said in John, "I am come that you might have meetings, meetings in abundance!" What matters is that our commitment to worship, rest, and celebration must be consistent with God's standards. Our ordering of our

---

2. Thomas Watson, *The Ten Commandments* (London: Banner of Truth Trust, 1970), 93.

priorities, our time with the family, or our commitment to care for others – all of these are signals to those around us that we are part of God's new society.

This will become more and more difficult as our societies drift towards secularism, but it will be an essential ingredient for the health of our souls and bodies, the health of our churches and perhaps too, the health of the societies we are able to influence for good.

Share some practical ideas of how we can make Sunday a day that is characterized by rest, refreshment, and celebration.

How do we avoid legalism on the one hand, and a drift towards expediency on the other?

---

3. The Identity of God's People – and the Danger of Compromise

How must Nehemiah have been feeling as he encountered a third area where promise had not been matched by performance? "Moreover, in those days I saw men of Judah who had married women from Ashdod, Ammon and Moab. Half of their children spoke the language of Ashdod or the language of one of the other peoples, and did not know how to speak the language of Judah" (v. 23).

Marrying people of other nations, as we have seen, was a threat to the solidarity and identity of God's own people. It was this that Nehemiah saw most clearly when he returned to Jerusalem. The danger to the next generation was that the Israelite identity would be eroded because the children could not understand God's Word, and their uniqueness as followers of the one Lord would gradually be dissolved.

It seemed to Nehemiah that everyone in Jerusalem was involved in such inter-marriage, including the hopelessly compromised leadership in the city. So again, he took what might seem to be drastic action, rebuking the leaders and making them promise not to pursue such disastrous compromise. "I rebuked them and called curses down on them. I beat some of the men and pulled out their hair. I made them take an oath in God's name and said, 'You are not to give your daughters in marriage to their sons, nor are you to take their daughters in marriage for your sons or for yourselves'" (v. 25).

Don't put your family at risk and don't put God's people at risk. As we've seen, there were special reasons why the Old Testament stresses this theme, which has to do with the identity of the nation and God's purposes of redemption. So the application of these verses needs to be handled with care and with sensitivity.

They are not to be used as arguments against cross-cultural marriage among Christians, nor are they to be used to make a Christian who has a non-Christian partner feel compromised, for reasons Paul explains in 1 Corinthians 7:12–16. Some Christians find themselves unavoidably in this situation, and they are encouraged here and also in 1 Peter 3 to see that this represents an important opportunity for them: ". . . if any of them do not believe the Word, they may be won over without words by the behaviour of their wives, when they see the purity and reverence of your lives" (1 Pet 3:1, 2). But nevertheless, Paul is very clear that, in making the decision to marry, the partner we Christians choose must "belong to the Lord" (1 Cor 7:39). He or she must be a believer. In other words, for Christians there is still a covenant relationship with God.

Paul's words in 2 Corinthians 6 are especially helpful as a commentary on this theme. He begins with a call in verse 14 not to be "yoked together with unbelievers," a picture borrowed from the book of Deuteronomy, where the law forbade ploughing a field using different kinds of animals working together – an ox and a donkey would pull at different speeds; they would be ineffective harnessed together.

This was one example of several instances in the Old Testament law where God's people were required to act consistently. Just as there should be no mismatched animals when ploughing a field, so there should be no mixing of crops in the field, and for the people themselves, no contamination with their pagan neighbours. It seems a legitimate application of Paul's call for consistent Christian living: he is calling us to avoid the wrong kind of marriage partnership.

If becoming a Christian means your whole view of life changes – different values, different ambitions, different ethical standards, and most importantly, a different authority in your life – how can you share your life intimately with someone outside of God's family? How can you be "at one"? "What does a believer have in common with an unbeliever?" (2 Cor 6:15). Painful as it might be initially, the Christian is called to avoid any close liaison, including marriage, which will compromise the distinctness of their calling.

Nehemiah chapter 13 reminds us of the special dangers of promising God one thing, but living something different. Reading this chapter will help us to see that God's people today need to keep alert to the danger of compromise. The call is simply this: make Jesus the number one priority. Seek first his kingdom. Don't just preach the Word, live the life.

We have seen from the New Testament teaching that the apostles encouraged Christians with non-Christian spouses to sustain their faithful witness and live obedient lives. How can we support fellow Christians who are in this situation?

Many people today would say that we need not be so strict in affirming the importance of a Christian young person marrying only another Christian. From the 2 Corinthians 6 passage, from other parts of the Bible, and from practical experience, try to provide clear reasons why the Christian position makes sense.

Nehemiah gets pretty physical in this chapter – throwing out Tobiah's household goods (v. 9), chasing away one of the priest's sons (v. 28), and beating some of the men and pulling out their hair (v. 25). He felt things pretty keenly. Do you think there are significant lessons here about our attitude to compromise and indifference – and how we should deal with sin today?

Further Study

Read Revelation 21 and identify the contrasts between the New Jerusalem – our eventual home – and the Jerusalem of Nehemiah's day.

Reflection and Response

Integrity, perseverance, and hope – these are the closing themes of this chapter, and they are basic to strengthening our "faith in the face of danger." Spend some time praying with others about each of these qualities, asking God to build them solidly into our lives.

Review of Section 5: Nehemiah 10 and 13

Before we complete our study of Nehemiah chapter 13, it would be good to reflect on three themes for our own Christian living.

1. Christian Integrity

The final chapter of Nehemiah could not be more relevant to the twenty-first century church. We face the constant temptation to compromise with the world. Its seductive appeal comes in many forms, pressurizing us to conform in relationships, business, sexuality, materialism, ambition, and lifestyle. But as God's new society, our task is to challenge the world, not conform to it. To do that we need the empowering of God's Spirit and the truth of God's Word.

The author Francis Schaeffer called Christians to live consistently with the word God has given, in the world God has made. As in the fifth century BC, the distinctness of God's people will result in effective witness to the God to whom we belong. We live our lives before a watching world.

As Peter reminds us, "Live such good lives among the pagans that, though they accuse you of doing wrong, they may see your good deeds and glorify God on the day he visits us" (1 Pet 2:12).

Having looked at these chapters, in what ways can our lives become an echo of the world rather than a challenge to its value system?

How can we help one another to respond to this call to Christian integrity?

---

2. Christian Perseverance

Comparing chapters 10 and 13 of Nehemiah reminds us of one of the most important gifts of the Spirit – the gift of perseverance. It is the ability, having put our hand to the plough, to keep cutting a straight furrow. As commentators rightly say about these chapters, they remind us that the church can take nothing for granted. The Reformers of the sixteenth century stressed that the church needs always to be reformed, and this will continue to be the case until we reach our home in heaven.

So we must call one another in the church of God to be constantly vigilant, constantly living under the authority of Scripture, constantly seeking the Spirit's help in our commitment to obey. Nehemiah was determined, as we see from his short prayers in chapter 13, that he would be remembered for faithfulness not failure. That's what we want, isn't it? Like Nehemiah, and like Paul, I would like my closing words to be:

> "I have fought the good fight, I have finished the race, I have kept the faith. Now there is in store for me a crown of righteousness, which the Lord, the righteous Judge, will award to me on that day – and not only to me, but also to all who have longed for his appearing." (2 Tim 4:7–8)

Can you think of examples of godly believers known to you, for whom these words of Paul are true? What do you think has been their secret?

Try to identify together the key disciplines in the Christian life that will help you not only run the race, but complete it.

---

3. Christian Hope

The story of Nehemiah is a story of human fickleness and of God's faithfulness. We began in Nehemiah's prayer in chapter 1 with the reminder of God's purposes: "If you return to me and obey my commands, then even if your exiled people are at the farthest horizon, I will gather them from there and bring them to the place I have chosen as a dwelling for my Name" (1:9). In part, that happened, but we have seen only a shadow of the ultimate reality of which that prayer speaks. By the close of Nehemiah 13, we have not yet seen the promised spiritual restoration. In AD 70, the Romans destroyed the walls and the temple once again. The story of the unfaithfulness of God's people is a recurring theme.

Something totally new would be required, as Jeremiah predicted in his promise of a new covenant. In Jesus himself, God would fulfil his promises to restore his people, not now defined by walls or a temple, not now restricted in its membership, but made up of men and women from every nation and tribe and tongue and people. It is in him that all of God's promises are finally fulfilled.

Right now, as C. S. Lewis observed, we Christians live in the "shadowlands." But it will not always be like that, and until we reach heaven, we need to live our lives with utter devotion to the Lord as a distinctive community honouring his name. We do so with our hearts and minds fixed on our eternal home, our destiny as the people of God.

John's vision in Revelation 21 of a New Jerusalem is surely the place to conclude. He sees a city, with its gates never shut (v. 25), with nothing impure entering (v. 27), with no enemies threatening it:

> . . . the Holy City, the new Jerusalem coming down out of heaven from God, prepared as a bride beautifully dressed for her husband. And I heard a loud voice from the throne saying, "Look! God's dwelling-place is now among the people, and he will dwell with them. They will be his people, and God himself will be with them and be their God. He will wipe every tear from their eyes. There will be no more death or mourning or crying or pain, for the old order of things has passed away." (Rev 21:2–4)

Even so, come, Lord Jesus!

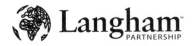

Langham Literature and its imprints are a ministry of Langham Partnership.

Langham Partnership is a global fellowship working in pursuit of the vision God entrusted to its founder John Stott –

to facilitate the growth of the church in maturity and Christ-likeness through raising the standards of biblical preaching and teaching.

Our vision is to see churches in the majority world equipped for mission and growing to maturity in Christ through the ministry of pastors and leaders who believe, teach and live by the Word of God.

Our mission is to strengthen the ministry of the Word of God through:
• nurturing national movements for biblical preaching
• fostering the creation and distribution of evangelical literature
• enhancing evangelical theological education
especially in countries where churches are under-resourced.

Our ministry

Langham Preaching partners with national leaders to nurture indigenous biblical preaching movements for pastors and lay preachers all around the world. With the support of a team of trainers from many countries, a multi-level programme of seminars provides practical training, and is followed by a programme for training local facilitators. Local preachers' groups and national and regional networks ensure continuity and ongoing development, seeking to build vigorous movements committed to Bible exposition.

Langham Literature provides majority world preachers, scholars and seminary libraries with evangelical books and electronic resources through publishing and distribution, grants and discounts. The programme also fosters the creation of indigenous evangelical books in many languages, through writer's grants, strengthening local evangelical publishing houses, and investment in major regional literature projects, such as one volume Bible commentaries like *The Africa Bible Commentary* and *The South Asia Bible Commentary*.

Langham Scholars provides financial support for evangelical doctoral students from the majority world so that, when they return home, they may train pastors and other Christian leaders with sound, biblical and theological teaching. This programme equips those who equip others. Langham Scholars also works in partnership with majority world seminaries in strengthening evangelical theological education. A growing number of Langham Scholars study in high quality doctoral programmes in the majority world itself. As well as teaching the next generation of pastors, graduated Langham Scholars exercise significant influence through their writing and leadership.

To learn more about Langham Partnership and the work we do visit **langham.org**